Survival

GLOBAL POLITICS AND STRATEGY

Volume 66 Number 1 | February–March 2024

'In 2022, Ukraine was able to make effective use of attrition and exploit the structural problems in the Russian war effort. In 2023, it was not able to repeat the success of 2022, though Russia too has failed to make any significant gains on the ground.'

Franz-Stefan Gady and Michael Kofman, Making Attrition Work: A Viable Theory of Victory for Ukraine, p. 11.

'In the nineteenth century, indigenous people relied on the courts to protect their equities and won important decisions. Their engagement over time with the United States judiciary, Congress and the executive branch could scarcely reverse a tragic fate or nullify the racist hostility of other Americans, but it did help them survive despite the odds.'

Steven Simon, Book Reviews: Politics and International Relations, p. 152.

'Zelenskyy, for his part, cannot afford to wait for Iran or any other medium power to reorient geopolitics. The trends running against him are broad-based and gathering momentum.'

John Raine, Ukraine vs Gaza, p. 177.

Survival

GLOBAL POLITICS AND STRATEGY

Volume 66 Number 1 | February–March 2024

Contents

On the cover
Ukrainian President
Volodymyr Zelenskyy
and US President Joe
Biden meet at the White
House in Washington DC
on 12 December 2023.

On the web
Visit www.iiss.org/
publications/survival
for brief notices on
new books on Politics
and International
Relations, Russia
and Eurasia, Africa,
and Deterrence and
Arms Control.

Survival **editors' blog**
For ideas and
commentary from
Survival editors and
contributors, visit
https://www.iiss.
org/online-analysis/
survival-online.

Survival

GLOBAL POLITICS AND STRATEGY

The International Institute for Strategic Studies

2121 K Street, NW | Suite 600 | Washington DC 20037 | USA
Tel +1 202 659 1490   Fax +1 202 659 1499   E-mail survival@iiss.org   Web www.iiss.org

Arundel House | 6 Temple Place | London | WC2R 2PG | UK
Tel +44 (0)20 7379 7676   Fax +44 (0)20 7836 3108   E-mail iiss@iiss.org

14th Floor, GFH Tower | Bahrain Financial Harbour | Manama | Kingdom of Bahrain
Tel +973 1718 1155   Fax +973 1710 0155   E-mail iiss-middleeast@iiss.org

9 Raffles Place | #49-01 Republic Plaza | Singapore 048619
Tel +65 6499 0055   Fax +65 6499 0059   E-mail iiss-asia@iiss.org

Pariser Platz 6A | 10117 Berlin | Germany
Tel +49 30 311 99 300   E-mail iiss-europe@iiss.org

Survival Online www.tandfonline.com/survival and www.iiss.org/publications/survival

Aims and Scope *Survival* is one of the world's leading forums for analysis and debate of international and strategic affairs. Shaped by its editors to be both timely and forward thinking, the journal encourages writers to challenge conventional wisdom and bring fresh, often controversial, perspectives to bear on the strategic issues of the moment. With a diverse range of authors, *Survival* aims to be scholarly in depth while vivid, well written and policy-relevant in approach. Through commentary, analytical articles, case studies, forums, review essays, reviews and letters to the editor, the journal promotes lively, critical debate on issues of international politics and strategy.

Editor **Dana Allin**
Managing Editor **Jonathan Stevenson**
Associate Editor **Carolyn West**
Editorial Assistant **Conor Hodges**
Production and Cartography **Alessandra Beluffi, Ravi Gopar, Jade Panganiban, James Parker, Kelly Verity**

Contributing Editors

William Alberque	Chester A. Crocker	Melissa K. Griffith	Irene Mia	Karen Smith
Målfrid Braut-	Bill Emmott	Emile Hokayem	Meia Nouwens	Angela Stent
Hegghammer	Franz-Stefan Gady	Nigel Inkster	Benjamin Rhode	Robert Ward
Aaron Connelly	Bastian Giegerich	Jeffrey Mazo	Ben Schreer	Marcus Willett
James Crabtree	Nigel Gould-Davies	Fenella McGerty	Maria Shagina	Lanxin Xiang

Published for the IISS by
Routledge Journals, an imprint of Taylor & Francis, an Informa business.

ISBN 978-1-032-80656-3 paperback / 978-1-003-49797-4 ebook

SUBMISSIONS

To submit an article, authors are advised to follow these guidelines:

- *Survival* articles are around 4,000–10,000 words long including endnotes. A word count should be included with a draft.
- All text, including endnotes, should be double-spaced with wide margins.
- Any tables or artwork should be supplied in separate files, ideally not embedded in the document or linked to text around it.
- All *Survival* articles are expected to include endnote references. These should be complete and include first and last names of authors, titles of articles (even from newspapers), place of publication, publisher, exact publication dates, volume and issue number (if from a journal) and page numbers. Web sources should include complete URLs and DOIs if available.
- A summary of up to 150 words should be included with the article. The summary should state the main argument clearly and concisely, not simply say what the article is about.

- A short author's biography of one or two lines should also be included. This information will appear at the foot of the first page of the article.

Please note that *Survival* has a strict policy of listing multiple authors in alphabetical order.

Submissions should be made by email, in Microsoft Word format, to survival@iiss.org. Alternatively, hard copies may be sent to *Survival*, IISS–US, 2121 K Street NW, Suite 801, Washington, DC 20037, USA.

The editorial review process can take up to three months. *Survival*'s acceptance rate for unsolicited manuscripts is less than 20%. *Survival* does not normally provide referees' comments in the event of rejection. Authors are permitted to submit simultaneously elsewhere so long as this is consistent with the policy of the other publication and the Editors of *Survival* are informed of the dual submission.

Readers are encouraged to comment on articles from the previous issue. Letters should be concise, no longer than 750 words and relate directly to the argument or points made in the original article.

Survival: Global Politics and Strategy (Print ISSN 0039-6338, Online ISSN 1468-2699) is published bimonthly for a total of 6 issues per year by Taylor & Francis Group, 4 Park Square, Milton Park, Abingdon, Oxon, OX14 4RN, UK. Periodicals postage paid (Permit no. 13095) at Brooklyn, NY 11256.

Airfreight and mailing in the USA by agent named World Container Inc., c/o BBT 150-15, 183rd Street, Jamaica, NY 11413, USA.

US Postmaster: Send address changes to Survival, World Container Inc., c/o BBT 150-15, 183rd Street, Jamaica, NY 11413, USA.

Subscription records are maintained at Taylor & Francis Group, 4 Park Square, Milton Park, Abingdon, OX14 4RN, UK.

Subscription information: For more information and subscription rates, please see tandfonline.com/pricing/journal/TSUR. Taylor & Francis journals are available in a range of different packages, designed to suit every library's needs and budget. This journal is available for institutional subscriptions with online-only or print & online options. This journal may also be available as part of our libraries, subject collections or archives. For more information on our sales packages, please visit librarianresources.taylorandfrancis.com.

For support with any institutional subscription, please visit help.tandfonline.com or email our dedicated team at subscriptions@tandf.co.uk.

Subscriptions purchased at the personal rate are strictly for personal, non-commercial use only. The reselling of personal subscriptions is prohibited. Personal subscriptions must be purchased with a personal cheque, credit card or BAC/wire transfer. Proof of personal status may be requested.

Back issues: Taylor & Francis Group retains a current and one-year back-issue stock of journals. Older volumes are held by our official stockists to whom all orders and enquiries should be addressed: Periodicals Service Company, 351 Fairview Avenue, Suite 300, Hudson, NY 12534, USA. Tel: +1 518 537 4700; email psc@periodicals.com.

Ordering information: To subscribe to the journal, please contact T&F Customer Services, Informa UK Ltd, Sheepen Place, Colchester, Essex, CO3 3LP, UK. Tel: +44 (0) 20 8052 2030; email subscriptions@tandf.co.uk.

Taylor & Francis journals are priced in USD, GBP and EUR (as well as AUD and CAD for a limited number of journals). All subscriptions are charged depending on where the end customer is based. If you are unsure which rate applies to you, please contact Customer Services. All subscriptions are payable in advance and all rates include postage. We are required to charge applicable VAT/GST on all print and online combination subscriptions, in addition to our online-only journals. Subscriptions are entered on an annual basis, i.e., January to December. Payment may be made by sterling

cheque, dollar cheque, euro cheque, international money order, National Giro or credit cards (Amex, Visa and Mastercard).

Disclaimer: The International Institute for Strategic Studies (IISS) and our publisher Informa UK Limited, trading as Taylor & Francis Group ('T&F'), make every effort to ensure the accuracy of all the information (the 'Content') contained in our publications. However, IISS and our publisher T&F, our agents and our licensors make no representations or warranties whatsoever as to the accuracy, completeness or suitability for any purpose of the Content. Any opinions and views expressed in this publication are the opinions and views of the authors, and are not the views of or endorsed by IISS or our publisher T&F. The accuracy of the Content should not be relied upon and should be independently verified with primary sources of information, and any reliance on the Content is at your own risk. IISS and our publisher T&F make no representations, warranties or guarantees, whether express or implied, that the Content is accurate, complete or up to date. IISS and our publisher T&F shall not be liable for any losses, actions, claims, proceedings, demands, costs, expenses, damages and other liabilities whatsoever or howsoever caused arising directly or indirectly in connection with, in relation to or arising out of the use of the Content. Full Terms & Conditions of access and use can be found at http://www.tandfonline.com/page/terms-and-conditions.

Informa UK Limited, trading as Taylor & Francis Group, grants authorisation for individuals to photocopy copyright material for private research use, on the sole basis that requests for such use are referred directly to the requestor's local Reproduction Rights Organization (RRO). The copyright fee is exclusive of any charge or fee levied. In order to contact your local RRO, please contact International Federation of Reproduction Rights Organizations (IFRRO), rue du Prince Royal, 87, B-1050 Brussels, Belgium; email ifrro@skynet.be; Copyright Clearance Center Inc., 222 Rosewood Drive, Danvers, MA 01923, USA; email info@copyright.com; or Copyright Licensing Agency, 90 Tottenham Court Road, London, W1P 0LP, UK; email cla@cla.co.uk. This authorisation does not extend to any other kind of copying, by any means, in any form, for any purpose other than private research use.

Submission information: See https://www.tandfonline.com/journals/tsur20

Advertising: See https://taylorandfrancis.com/contact/advertising/

Permissions: See help.tandfonline.com/Librarian/s/article/Permissions

All Taylor & Francis Group journals are printed on paper from renewable sources by accredited partners.

February–March 2024

THE ADELPHI SERIES

PLANNING FOR PROTRACTION

A Historically Informed Approach to Great-power War and Sino-US Competition

'Iskander Rehman brings fresh insights into what the Eisenhower administration called "broken-back warfare" – combat that is expansive in scale, scope and duration, with cycles of escalation. This excellent study examines both US and Chinese military writings in the context of broader military history. It is reminiscent of George H. Quester's *Deterrence Before Hiroshima* in prompting reconsideration of comfortably situated concepts.'

KORI SCHAKE, Senior Fellow and Director of Foreign and Defense Policy Studies, American Enterprise Institute; former Deputy Director of Policy Planning, US Department of State

Iskander Rehman

As Sino-US relations have deteriorated, concerns have grown in Washington over its ability to defeat China in a major conflict. A confrontation between such peer competitors would likely become a protracted war of attrition drawing on all dimensions of national power, but this reality has yet to receive a sufficient degree of analytical attention.

In this *Adelphi* book, Iskander Rehman provides a historically informed and empirically grounded study of protracted great-power war, its core drivers and characteristics, and an examination of the elements that have most often determined a competitor's long-term strategic performance. A detailed analysis of the contemporary Sino-US rivalry assesses how both parties might fare in the event of a protracted war, while highlighting some of its key significant differentiating aspects – most notably its nuclear and cyber dimensions.

IISS
THE INTERNATIONAL INSTITUTE
FOR STRATEGIC STUDIES

www.iiss.org/publications/adelphi

Making Attrition Work: A Viable Theory of Victory for Ukraine

Franz-Stefan Gady and Michael Kofman

As the Russia–Ukraine war enters its third year, Ukraine faces a daunting task: how to restore its military advantage. The 2023 summer offensive, which dragged into autumn, was unsuccessful. Planning for the offensive appears to have been overly optimistic and poorly connected to how the Ukrainian armed forces actually fight, despite numerous analyses warning that the operation would prove costly and difficult, and that manoeuvre warfare was unlikely to attain a quick breakthrough against a well-prepared defence.[1]

Conditions are not propitious for another major ground offensive in 2024. Our observations during field trips to Ukraine over the past year indicate that, to maximise Ukraine's chances of eventual victory, Western countries need to recognise that the driving engine of Ukraine's effectiveness has been a destruction-centred approach, resulting in high levels of attrition – that is, reducing an enemy's capacity to fight by inflicting higher losses in personnel and materiel than one's own side is suffering, which privileges firepower over mobility and direct attack or prepared defence over flanking action. Attempts at manoeuvre against a prepared defence have consistently floundered, especially in the absence of a decisive force advantage. While manoeuvre is still relevant on the battlefield, it will need a lot of help from attrition to bear fruit.

Franz-Stefan Gady is IISS Consulting Senior Fellow for Cyber Power and Future Conflict, and an Adjunct Senior Fellow at the Center for a New American Security. **Michael Kofman** is a Senior Fellow in the Russia and Eurasia Program at the Carnegie Endowment for International Peace.

Survival | vol. 66 no. 1 | February–March 2024 | pp. 7–24   https://doi.org/10.1080/00396338.2024.2309068

The West should focus on resourcing Ukraine's ability to establish a decisive advantage in fires – meaning, typically, tube and rocket artillery, battlefield strike drones, long-range precision-strike systems and support by tactical aviation. No less important, the West needs to help Ukraine scale its capacity to employ units so that it can exploit that advantage in offensive operations. Western countries should also help Ukraine ramp up industrial production of those capabilities that provide the greatest advantages in an attritional war. The West will need to be appreciative of Ukrainian force structure and military culture, as well as the challenges posed by an increasingly mobilised military, which means avoiding the temptation to try to convert the Ukrainian military to a more Western, manoeuvre-centred way of fighting.

A war of attrition

The more we know about the history of this war, the clearer it becomes how much was contingent, and how little was in fact overdetermined. Russia's initial invasion was a high-risk operation, premised on the assumption that a long war could be avoided through the combination of a subversion campaign and a decisive decapitation strike against the Ukrainian government.[2] In essence, the Russian concept of operations was driven by political assumptions, and therefore involved the use of forces in a manner that did not reflect how the Russian military trains and organises to fight in larger-scale combat operations. The invasion instead assumed that Russian forces could paralyse Ukrainian decision-making, isolate Ukraine's armed formations and quickly advance across the vast country without meeting sustained resistance. The plans and objectives were also kept secret from the Russian troops until the final days or hours, leaving them materially and psychologically unready for a major campaign.

The first few days saw a confluence of events. Ukrainian units deployed on short notice, encountering streaming columns of Russian forces that were trying to meet compressed timetables. The decisive factor in many of these battles was not Western-provided weaponry but rather artillery. Russian forces were dispersed, unable to mass as they attempted to rapidly advance along divergent routes, and at a firepower disadvantage despite having overall superiority in fires.[3] The Russian invasion force was brittle, consisting of perhaps 150,000 troops, with a third of it composed of mobilised personnel from the Luhansk and Donetsk people's republics, and auxiliaries from RosGvardia, Russia's National Guard.

Following a series of defeats, Russian forces regrouped and pursued a campaign in the Donbas, offsetting a deficit in personnel with an artillery fire advantage of 12:1. They fired an average of 20,000 shells per day during this time period, and likely averaged 15,000 over the course of 2022.[4] Ukrainian casualties rose as Ukrainian forces were outgunned and ran low on ammunition. At this stage, Western assistance became crucial. Various types of tube artillery and long-range precision-strike systems entered the war. Most importantly, Western ammunition enabled Ukraine to sustain defensive fire so as to exhaust the Russian offensive in the Donbas and conduct localised counter-offensives to maintain pressure. Although Russia's sieges of Mariupol and Severodonetsk were ultimately successful, Russian forces paid a steep price. The decisive factor in the Russian campaign was artillery firepower, which allowed the Russian military to establish localised advantages in the correlation of forces, despite being disadvantaged in personnel overall.

Ukraine then retook the initiative, launching two major offensives of its own in late summer and autumn 2022. Attrition worked to its advantage. Ukraine had mobilised and substantially expanded the size of its forces, whereas Russia was trying to fight the war at peacetime strength. Russia lacked the forces to stabilise a front stretching more than 1,600 kilometres. In Kharkiv, Russia had only a thinly manned line with an incohesive mixture of units. The bulk of those units were the remnants of the Western Group of Forces, in some places at 25% strength, with low morale due to desertions.[5] Ukrainian forces broke through at Kharkiv, leading to a Russian rout. But the decisive factor was attrition, which forced the Russian military to choose between defending Kherson and reinforcing Kharkiv.

The Russian military deployed airborne units in Kherson, prioritising that region with a relatively well-prepared defence. The initial Ukrainian offensive was unsuccessful, prompting the replacement of the commander in charge of the operation. Entrenched behind multiple lines peppered with minefields, Russian units held in September, yielding little territory. The geometry of the battlefield was highly favourable to Ukraine, with Russian units separated from their logistical-support network by the Dnipro River. Months of High Mobility Artillery Rocket System (HIMARS) strikes had further reduced the Russian supply line to one bridge across the Kakhovka Dam and a network of ferries. Although Russian forces contained a renewed Ukrainian offensive in October, Moscow was compelled to retreat in order to preserve the force, as the attritional battle strongly favoured Ukraine.

Kherson was a portent of the challenge to come in the Ukrainian counter-offensive of 2023. Ukraine struggled to break through a prepared defence.[6] Months of HIMARS strikes constrained Russian logistics, but they did not enable a breakthrough, and Russian forces were ultimately able to withdraw. They were at their weakest point over the winter, but the Ukrainian army was also in no condition to press the advantage. Having run through mobilised personnel from Luhansk and Donetsk, Moscow was forced to mobilise another 300,000 men, which served to stabilise their lines. Meanwhile, a grinding battle at Bakhmut, led by the Wagner Group, turned into a bloody and politically symbolic fight. Wagner eventually captured Bakhmut in May due to three factors: the Russian airborne held their flanks to prevent counter-attacks; Russian commanders had access to a large supply of convicts from the Russian prison system to use as assault infantry; and most importantly Russia enjoyed a fires advantage of 5:1 for much of the battle. Both sides thought that attrition favoured them.

Based on our research, Ukraine enjoyed a favourable loss ratio over Russia of up to 1:4 in total casualties during the nine-month battle, but the Russian forces that were fighting as part of Wagner were likely 70% convicts. Bakhmut thus immersed Ukrainian units in a fight in which Ukraine had the advantage on the basis of the attrition ratio, but which would pit its more experienced and valuable soldiers against Russia's relatively expendable ones. The city itself had little strategic value. Wagner was particularly effective in urban terrain owing to its ruthless employment of expendable assault infantry. As the battle dragged on, the rest of the Russian military used the time to dig in, entrenching and laying down minefields across much of the southern and northern fronts. Buoyed by mobilisation, the

Russian military launched its own winter offensive in late January by way of a series of localised attacks across a broad front.

This effort proved unsuccessful because the Russian forces were unable to achieve a sufficient advantage to break through, the force quality being too low to coordinate attacks in large formations. Many of the attacks were undertaken by platoon-sized units, which quickly drew Ukrainian fire and were defeated. The fires advantage Russian forces enjoyed in 2022 also started to deteriorate. This was not due primarily to HIMARS strikes, which forced a reorganisation of the Russian logistical system, but rather to the fact that Russia lacked the ammunition reserves to sustain the volume of fire reached in 2022. Those deficits began to force doctrinal adaptation in the Russian military, with greater emphasis on strike drones and more precise types of munitions.

This brief, circumscribed account does not explore the air war or maritime operations, but it does highlight the importance of force management, terrain and establishing a fires advantage, and the struggle by both sides to effectively employ their forces in offensive operations. With the exception of an initial manoeuvre-and-strike phase, which failed for conceptual and political reasons, the war has been characterised by attritional fighting and set-piece battles. In 2022, Ukraine was able to make effective use of attrition and exploit the structural problems in the Russian war effort. In 2023, it was not able to repeat the success of 2022, though Russia too has failed to make any significant gains on the ground.

Ukraine's 2023 offensive

Ukraine's offensive was freighted with unrealistic expectations, but the fact remains that summer 2023 presented a good opportunity to inflict a strategic defeat on Russia. Russian forces were low on ammunition and lacked offensive potential. It was reasonable to think that Ukraine could establish an advantage in artillery fire, and the risk of a Russian counter-offensive was low. Western support, which has been essential to Ukraine's war effort, was also likely to peak in summer 2023. The United States was burning through its stockpile of ammunition, while European states had failed to ramp up munitions production in 2022 and were just beginning to make the required investments, with lacklustre results. With elections looming in 2024, the political headwinds in Western capitals also suggested that funding to support Ukraine would decline following this operation. The US borrowed ammunition from South Korea, and other Western countries made efforts to contribute as part of a crash train-and-equip programme for Ukrainian forces. All told, the West trained and equipped nine brigades for the offensive. Ukraine would field several additional brigades from the armed forces and national guard, organised under two corps, and a reserve task force.

Ukraine had no risk-free options, but its strategy incorporated several choices and trade-offs, some of which compounded risk. Newly trained brigades, with just a few months of training, would take the lead in the assault, while more experienced units were kept fighting at Bakhmut. Ukraine also split its forces and artillery along three axes – Bakhmut, Velyka Novosilka and Tokmak – in hopes of pinning down Russian forces. Essentially, there were three offensives, which would pressure Russian forces such that they could not redeploy forces to one front without weakening another. In retrospect, the value of a prepared defence was underestimated, and Ukrainian forces could not attain the requisite advantage to break through along any of the operational directions selected. Western countries provided long-range air-launched cruise missiles in advance of the operation, but these capabilities did not prove decisive.

Whether Ukraine had sufficient breaching equipment, mine-clearing assets and air defence is still debated. But the more salient fact is that mobilisation had helped refill personnel levels within the Russian military and yielded more than 70 additional motor-rifle regiments, among other units.[7] Consequently, Russian force density was much higher relative to terrain held. Furthermore, Russian engineering brigades prepared defences with digging machines and cement, using bunkers and towns as strong points. In the south, along the Orikhiv–Tokmak axis, the Russian military established multiple defensive lines and held the high ground. Russian units focused on manning the first line of defence and conducted counter-attacks to prevent Ukrainian forces from gathering momentum. The challenge to Ukraine – involving an established defence, a high force-density-to-terrain ratio and unfavourable geometry – was much greater than it had been in Kherson. In terms of the condition of Russian forces, the situation was practically the opposite of the one that had prevailed in Kharkiv during Ukraine's break-through in September 2022.

The initial Ukrainian breaching effort in June failed. New units made common mistakes with respect to planning, coordinating artillery fire with assaults, orienting at night and employing breaching equipment, and in a few cases had engaged in unfortunate friendly-fire incidents early in the attack. Moreover, Ukrainian brigades could generate at most a few reinforced companies on the offence, backed by artillery. This meant that a brigade-level attack was in practice two reinforced companies advancing, with perhaps one in reserve. Ukraine was deploying combat power onto the battlefield in small packets, unable to coordinate formations at larger scale. Western equipment helped save lives, and proved much more survivable than comparable Russian kit,

Western equipment was hardly a game-changer

but by itself it was hardly a game-changer. In fact, more experienced units that stepped in after the failed initial assault, without Western equipment, performed better in both offensive and defensive tasks, demonstrating that while capability matters, experience and leadership also figure significantly into the equation. An advantage in artillery fire of between 3:2 and 2:1 yielded little better than overall parity, not enough to shock or suppress Russian formations, which anticipated and defended the main axis of the Ukrainian advance.

Subsequently, the Ukrainian military changed tactics, stressing dismounted-infantry attacks and seeking to attain an advantage in artillery fire sufficient to suppress Russian batteries. Much of the combat shifted to individual tree lines, typically at the level of platoons and occasionally that of reinforced companies. This approach reduced losses and preserved equipment, but did not lead to a breakthrough. Ukraine was able to breach the first Russian defensive line in the south but exhausted its offensive capacity by October without reaching its minimal objective of Tokmak. Ukraine also stuck with the overall strategy of splitting forces in three directions and keeping some of its better units in a sustained counter-attack at Bakhmut that yielded little.[8] Russia had enough reserves to rotate in airborne regiments by September and generated additional combat power sufficient to launch its own offensive in Avdiivka in October. The Russian offensive in Avdiivka equally failed to achieve a breakthrough, but it demonstrated that Russia had regenerated sufficient combat power to try to retake the initiative, and sufficient reserves to stop a Ukrainian breakthrough that year.

If Ukraine's summer offensive fell short of its objectives, it was hardly a disaster. Ukraine retained much of the equipment it had been allocated while inflicting significant losses on defending Russian forces. Tactically, it was closer to a draw. The initial attack failed due to a combination of planning choices, force-employment issues, a shortage of enablers and most importantly a lack of a clear fires advantage relative to a well-prepared defence. The West did fail to provide available counters that could have negated some of the Russian advantages, such as long-range strike against Russian helicopter bases. But the narrative that the offensive failed solely because the West failed to provide sufficient equipment to Ukraine lacks explanatory power, especially since Ukraine did not run out of equipment during the offensive and could not employ it at scale from the outset.

In retrospect, what is notable about the offensive is how convention-ally it was planned. It assumed an assault could breach Russian lines relatively quickly, and then be exploited with reserve forces.[9] This line of thinking discounted the presence of Russia's layered defences, persis-tent drone-based surveillance and panoply of capabilities that could deny manoeuvre. Given that Ukraine lacked a decisive superiority in the overall correlation of forces, the errant assumptions likely stemmed from the inor-dinate influence of the Western manoeuvrist school of thought, whereby the cognitive impact and shock of a combined-arms assault was supposed to force Russian units to withdraw from the first line, enabling a rapid breach and obviating the need to inflict high levels of attrition to set the conditions for success. In fact, the course of the war indicates that Ukraine and its Western backers did not sufficiently appreciate the importance of attrition as an enabler of manoeuvre, and that of a firepower advantage over combined-arms integration. Manoeuvrist tenets, which projected strong cognitive effects from manoeuvre, did not prove out in Ukraine's offensive, and indeed have not been validated over the two-year span of the Russia–Ukraine war.

Air superiority and fire control

The war has played out in a largely air-denied or air-contested environment. Nevertheless, Russian Aerospace Forces have enjoyed greater freedom of action than their Ukrainian counterpart and employed stand-off strikes to some effect. Tactical aviation – namely, American-made F-16s – or a much larger set of long-range strike capabilities are important factors, but by themselves they were unlikely to make the crucial difference. Ukrainian force structure and doctrine are not designed around attainment of air superiority or the need for substantial air-delivered fires, and some of the challenges posed by Russia's defences did not have obvious air-power solutions.

There is a tendency to treat air power as talismanic. But unstated assumptions about air power or long-range strike are often baked into expectations for what they might achieve. While Ukraine is steadily acquiring F-16 fighter aircraft and training to use them, this transition is a multiyear process. The fighters will eventually help Ukraine employ more Western strike capabilities and contest Russian air power, but having Western aircraft does not secure the ability to attain and maintain air superiority in an air-denied environment.

There is much a military would have to adjust with respect to how air power is employed, its organisational capacity and how operations are planned to effectively integrate air and land operations, and to realise the benefits of air power most associated with US achievements. Presuming sufficient kit would easily translate into that level of operational capability is especially problematic against a military, such as Russia's, with an extensive network of integrated air defences and a large fleet of tactical aircraft. It is therefore unsurprising and appropriate that current discussions in Ukraine centre less on conventional air superiority and more on the advantages derived from the employment of drones at the tactical level and as part of long-range strike campaigns.[10] This is a productive way to think about the sort of strike-support roles drones can play, and their ability to offset deficits in other capabilities.

The 'deep battle' notion, advanced by some, that Ukraine might have attained fire control – that is, the ability to strike critical Russian targets far behind Russian lines to facilitate a breakthrough – had it been able to advance within range of Russian ground lines of communication also seems unconvincing. This technology-centred theory of success made little sense: if it had been possible to achieve deep-battle effects by leveraging long-range strike capabilities, the offensive would not have been necessary in the first place. In the event, fire control via long-range precision strike was not practicable, and the persistent intelligence, surveillance and reconnaissance capabilities, magazine depth and other requirements needed to establish it at longer ranges were not attainable. Furthermore, long-range precision strikes were poorly coordinated with attacks along the front line, further reducing their tactical impact. Where Ukrainian forces excelled was in delegating HIMARS systems to engage Russian artillery and high-value targets close to the front line. This leveraged qualitative superiority in fires to establish some degree of advantage. However, in most battles in Ukraine, each side has been able to range the other's ground lines of communication, command and control, and forward logistics, with the lines often separated by a few kilometres. With rare exceptions, the combatants could not control the engagement via fires, resulting in attritional warfare that could last weeks or months.

While it makes sense for Ukraine to pursue localised air superiority and contest Russian air power, expectations about how quickly such efforts might produce meaningful results should be low. A long-term strategy should incorporate these efforts, but should not assume that they will be decisive or serve as centrepieces of the approach. Although fire control appears impractical, Ukraine could instead cultivate an expanded long-range strike capability for targeting key supporting elements of the Russian war effort far beyond tactical depths. In particular, low-cost drones in high volumes might prove more useful in degrading the Russian air advantage than in directly contesting it, and could anchor a sustained Ukrainian strike campaign over the course of 2024. They should not be viewed as a substitute for close battle, however. No matter how abundant, long-range strike capability is not likely to force a collapse of Russian positions without another ground offensive. In sum, it is necessary but not sufficient, and no theory of victory should be based on these means alone.

Making attrition work

The most recent offensive raises the question of whether the West should emphasise a combined-arms, manoeuvre-based approach, or focus instead on helping Ukraine attain advantage via a destruction-based approach, especially given what is likely to be a prolonged attritional phase. The course of the war illustrates that manoeuvre will have to be earned, and that integration and simultaneity – basically, the key virtues of combined-arms operations – are not only difficult to achieve but also unlikely to produce breakthroughs under the conditions prevailing in Ukraine. Rather, the focus needs to be first and foremost on the attritional destruction of Russia's forces by firepower in both the close and deep battles to pave the way for manoeuvre. Ukraine, in short, needs to embrace a destruction-centred approach for the next stage of the war, which may in time enable manoeuvre to be more successful.

Attrition is a more dependable approach in part because the force quality required to execute combined-arms operations at scale is often difficult to maintain and reconstitute later in a conventional war. The Ukrainian armed forces have had to undergo cycles of reconstituting and rebuilding formations, often after losing more experienced soldiers and leaders to attrition. New units often consist of mobilised personnel, officers from other formations, and those who were promoted in grade, most without any professional military education. The emphasis therefore has to be on the fundamentals to build planning capacity within battalion and brigade staffs. This is required before higher levels of coordination are possible and instilling a major doctrinal evolution into a traditionally fires-centred military is feasible.

Furthermore, Ukraine's principal problem in the 2023 offensive was not an inability to conduct combined-arms manoeuvre. While it is true the new brigades trained by Western countries struggled to coordinate combat arms, this was ancillary rather than central to the offensive's failure. Accordingly, it is incorrect to conclude that Ukrainian forces could not succeed because they could not fight like a Western military, or that fighting like a Western military doctrinally requires air superiority, without which success is impossible. In fact, Ukraine made progress by trying to gain better positions, fighting for relative fires advantage that reduced overall losses, and made Russia pay a high price to defend terrain. Fighting like a Western military is not necessarily a recipe for success in this war. As many Ukrainian soldiers have suggested, the operating environment is such that some Western tactics and techniques appear unsuitable or dated.

Restoring Ukraine's advantage

In a prior article discussing the course of the war in 2022, we assessed that combined-arms training and precision-strike systems would not prove sufficient to escape attrition in the coming offensive.[11] Assuming Ukraine and the West now accept the unavoidability of a long war, both need to settle on a long-term strategy to effectively defend against Russian offensive operations, reconstitute Ukrainian forces and maintain pressure on the Russian military with the goal of restoring a battlefield advantage to Ukrainian armed forces. The strategy should cast 2024 as a pivotal year, with an eye to restoring the ability to conduct a successful offensive in 2025.

At this point, Russia has several material advantages. It is likely to retain an artillery-fire edge over the course of the year and beyond. Russia will also continue regenerating combat power, recruiting more than 10,000 troops per month. It will probably hold the strategic initiative along much of the 1,000 km front line and expand its strike campaign against Ukraine given increased production of drones and cruise missiles. Moreover, Moscow is now set to spend 6% of GDP on defence – a significant increase – and the real figure may be closer to 8%.[12] Its apparent intent is to overwhelm Ukraine through defence-industrial mobilisation and sustained regeneration of combat forces.

The most effective way for Ukraine to rebuild its advantage is to mount an effective defence in depth, which will reduce Ukraine's losses and ammunition requirements. At present, Russia holds the defensive advantage, on account of dedicated engineering brigades, machinery and the capacity to fortify quickly, as well as extensive minefields and sophisticated minelaying systems, including those capable of distance mining. A better defence would also permit Ukraine to restructure its force deployments, rotate brigades and free up parts of the military for reconstitution.

Ukraine will also have to replenish its force. Based on our field research, Ukraine's average soldier appears to be in his 40s, which is ill-suited for certain combat tasks. Ukrainian leadership needs to review policies on the ages of those conscripted. The West can assist by scaling up training programmes, which need to be adjusted on the basis of lessons learned in the 2023 offensive and Ukrainian experience in this war. Within Ukraine, expanded facilities and training ranges will be needed to rotate units off and onto the front line. Further, units that have been on the front lines since the beginning of the war – particularly those at Bakhmut – need rest and recuperation.

More broadly, Ukraine's military requires recapitalisation. Ukraine and its Western backers need to increase industrial capacity and output of key systems in order to ensure that Ukraine will have the requisite fires advantage. For supporting countries, the challenge is to significantly increase production of artillery ammunition and air-defence interceptors. Our field research indicates that Ukraine will need around 75,000–90,000 artillery shells per month to sustain the war defensively, and more than double that – 200,000–250,000 – for a major offensive. At this stage, the Western coalition depends mostly on US stocks to sustain the lower range of this figure and does not have the ammunition to support a major offensive next year. Ukraine can reduce its requirements for artillery ammunition by significantly increasing production of strike drones, both first-person-view drones for use in close battle and long-range strike drones to target Russian critical infrastructure. To do this, Ukraine will have to resolve several financing, contracting and industrial-capacity issues. The West, for its part, will need to support Ukraine in procuring or developing munitions to use with drones, as such munitions from other sources are in short supply. Ukraine's indigenous ability to maintain and repair Western armoured fighting vehicles and artillery is growing, and the West should work to advance the localisation of maintenance, parts replacement and production of strike systems.

Naturally, defence and reconstitution by themselves are not enough, and Ukraine will have to be careful about being drawn into costly battles like Bakhmut, which tend to lead to a sunk-costs mentality. These may be politically symbolic, but they trade short-term gain for strategic costs that hamper reconstitution. At this stage of the war, the West is neither expecting nor desirous of fleeting or isolated battlefield victories for the continuation of its support. Instead, Ukraine should plan for and execute strike campaigns – for example, against the Russian Black Sea Fleet, Russian air bases in Crimea or key supporting infrastructure. Heading into 2024, it is clear that the optimal strategy is one that avoids a costly stalemate, or worse, a mounting Russian advantage that leads to Ukraine's defeat. Both Ukraine and the Western countries involved retain good options, but success will require better alignment on strategy.

*   *   *

We recognise that much of our analysis represents an incomplete first draft of military history. Other analysts and historians will undoubtedly revise and improve our understanding of this war. But it does seem fairly clear that the war has seen prolonged phases in which the ability to manoeuvre has been earned chiefly through extensive attrition and the destruction of the enemy's capacity rather than through cognitive effects or effective employment of combined arms. Modern forms of long-range precision strike have helped Ukraine to interdict or suppress Russia's logistical nodes, but they have not established fire control beyond tactical ranges or circumvented the need for close battle. We appreciate that these results may be due to the specific context of this war, and analysts should be careful in trying to translate observations about the Russia–Ukraine war in particular into lessons learned about the character of contemporary war in general.

While Western countries should continue to help Ukrainian forces improve their overall quality and their ability to scale up combined-arms operations, prevailing conditions in Ukraine still favour attritional and positional approaches rather than those suitable for manoeuvre warfare.[13] The operative factor is attrition, inflicted primarily through artillery and strike drones. The West is therefore best served by focusing on resourcing Ukraine's fires-centred approach and helping Ukraine scale offensive operations to exploit a fires advantage when it is attained. This may be impossible to achieve via quantity, but it can be done through a combination of means which altogether add up to meaningful superiority in support of an offensive. These two factors should drive investment in drones to offset shortages of artillery ammunition, cheaper precision-strike capabilities, and electronic warfare to help restore mobility to the front line and reduce current Russian advantages in drone systems.

Ukraine's military leadership appears keen to embrace technological innovation and tactical adaptation, and to rebuild the force's combat potential. These objectives will take time to achieve, but it is clear that Ukraine's military recognises the scale of the challenge and the need to move out as soon as possible in 2024. This will be a long war requiring a long-term outlook in strategy, but also timely decision-making. Despite the high stakes, it has become less clear that Washington and European capitals can muster the political will to see Ukraine through this war. The fact remains that Ukraine and the West enjoy the overall advantage in resources, and attrition can prove an important part of their theory of victory.

Notes

[1] See Franz-Stefan Gady and Michael Kofman, 'Ukraine's Strategy of Attrition', *Survival*, vol. 65, no. 2, April–May 2023, pp. 7–22; Michael Kofman and Rob Lee, 'Beyond Ukraine's Offensive', *Foreign Affairs*, 10 May 2023, https://www.foreignaffairs.com/ukraine/russia-war-beyond-ukraines-offensive; and Rob Lee and Michael Kofman, 'How the Battle for the Donbas Shaped Ukraine's Success', Foreign Policy Research Institute, 23 December 2022, https://www.fpri.org/article/2022/12/how-the-battle-for-the-donbas-shaped-ukraines-success/.

[2] See Jack Watling, Oleksandr V. Danylyuk and Nick Reynolds, 'Preliminary Lessons from Russia's Unconventional Operations During the Russo-Ukrainian War, February 2022–2023', RUSI, 29 March 2023, https://rusi.org/explore-our-research/publications/special-resources/preliminary-lessons-russias-unconventional-operations-during-russo-ukrainian-war-february-2022.

[3] See *ibid.*; and Mykhaylo Zabrodskyi et al., 'Preliminary Lessons in Conventional Warfighting from Russia's Invasion of Ukraine: February–July 2022', RUSI, 30 November 2022, https://rusi.org/explore-our-research/publications/special-resources/preliminary-lessons-conventional-warfighting-russias-invasion-ukraine-february-july-2022.

[4] See Jack Watling and Nick Reynolds, 'Ukraine at War: Paving the Road

from Survival to Victory', RUSI, 4 July 2022, https://www.rusi.org/explore-our-research/publications/special-resources/ukraine-war-paving-road-survival-victory.

5   See Mari Saito, Maria Tsvetkova and Anton Zverev, 'Abandoned Russian Base Holds Secrets of Retreat in Ukraine', Reuters, 26 October 2022, https://www.reuters.com/investigates/special-report/ukraine-crisis-russia-base/.

6   See Isabelle Khurshudyan et al., 'Inside the Ukrainian Counteroffensive that Shocked Putin and Reshaped the War', Washington Post, 29 December 2022, https://www.washingtonpost.com/world/2022/12/29/ukraine-offensive-kharkiv-kherson-donetsk/.

7   According to the Conflict Intelligence Team, a total of 123 military units were established, including 77 motor-rifle regiments and 18 separate motor-rifle battalions. See 'As Part of the Mobilization, More than 120 New Military Units Were Created in Russia. A Third of Those Called Up Were Sent to Personnel Units – To Make Up for Combat Losses', Meduza, 5 October 2023, https://meduza.io/feature/2023/10/05/v-ramkah-mobilizatsii-v-rossii-sozdali-bolee-120-novyh-voinskih-chastey-tret-prizvannyh-otpravili-v-kadrovye-chasti-vospolnyat-boevye-poteri.

8   See Michael Kofman and Rob Lee, 'Perseverance and Adaptation: Ukraine's Counteroffensive at Three Months', War on the Rocks, 4 September 2023, https://warontherocks.com/2023/09/perseverance-and-adaptation-ukraines-counteroffensive-at-three-months/.

9   See 'Miscalculations, Divisions Marked Offensive Planning by U.S., Ukraine', Washington Post, 4 December 2023, https://www.washingtonpost.com/world/2023/12/04/ukraine-counteroffensive-us-planning-russia-war/.

10 See Valery Zaluzhny, 'The Commander-in-Chief of Ukraine's Armed Forces on How to Win the War', The Economist, 1 November 2023, https://www.economist.com/by-invitation/2023/11/01/the-commander-in-chief-of-ukraines-armed-forces-on-how-to-win-the-war.

11 Gady and Kofman, 'Ukraine's Strategy of Attrition'.

12 See Alexandra Prokopenko, 'Putin's Unsustainable Spending Spree', Foreign Affairs, 8 January 2024, https://www.foreignaffairs.com/russian-federation/putins-unsustainable-spending-spree.

13 We define manoeuvre operations or warfare at the tactical level of war as the combination of rapid movement with firepower. As Amos C. Fox explains, 'modern maneuver warfare has two goals: (1) to achieve a psychological impact on an adversary – to create panic, or cognitive paralysis, forcing the enemy's will to resist to collapse; and (2) to gain and maintain a position of relative advantage in relation to a belligerent. Creating confusion (a cognitive effect) and disorganization (a physical effect) are subordinate goals of maneuver warfare that contribute to the concept's overarching aims. The idea of defeating the enemy through the most economic use of force is closely aligned with both of

these goals.' Positional warfare, he continues, 'can be defined as the use of force – through tactics, firepower or movement – to move an opponent from one position to another for further exploitation or to deny them access to an area for further exploitation – while attrition warfare can be defined as the methodical use of battle or shaping operations to erode or destroy a belligerent's equipment, personnel and resources at a pace greater than they can replenish their losses.' Amos C. Fox, 'A Solution Looking for a Problem: Illuminating Misconceptions in Maneuver-warfare Doctrine', US Army Maneuver Center of Excellence, Fall 2017, https://www.moore.army.mil/armor/earmor/content/issues/2017/Fall/4Fox17.pdf.

America Needs a Realistic Ukraine Debate

Christopher S. Chivvis

On the eve of the war's third year, Ukraine's vaunted counter-offensive has ended in stalemate. Ukraine may in fact lose ground this year. Political developments in the United States have meanwhile cast doubt on the sustainability of American support. While the Biden administration repeats the mantra of 'for as long as it takes', Republicans in Congress are indicating that it has already taken too long. In the House of Representatives, a hard core of MAGA Republicans has blocked the next tranche of military aid, ostensibly requiring draconian changes to US border policies in exchange for any concessions. There may be a majority in both houses of Congress favouring Ukraine aid in principle, but in practice Republicans have shown that it is not a top priority. Moreover, the increasingly plausible prospect that Donald Trump will return to the White House a year from now portends a dramatic turn away from Ukraine and into the unknown.

Facing this prospect, there is an understandable response on the internationalist centre-left to catastrophise and link Ukraine's defeat with the collapse of international order and end of American democracy itself. It would be more constructive, however, to assess how we ended up where we are now, after two full years of war with so few options to bring the fighting to an end and so little intellectual effort focused on

Christopher S. Chivvis is the director of the American Statecraft Program at the Carnegie Endowment for International Peace, and recently served as national intelligence officer for Europe in the US National Intelligence Council.

Survival | vol. 66 no. 1 | February–March 2024 | pp. 25–40   https://doi.org/10.1080/00396338.2024.2309071

developing realistic options for negotiations, ceasefires or other ways that the human and financial costs of the war might be reduced and the fighting halted. Revulsion against Russia's murderous treatment of Ukrainian civilians has naturally intensified the emotional content of the debate, making this difficult. But such an assessment might even yield some clues to explain the apparent precariousness of constitutional democracy in America.

A healthy democracy ought to be able to develop and debate its national-security options honestly, openly and vigorously. This has not been the case when it comes to Ukraine. The American debate is instead polarised between supporting Ukraine 'as long as it takes' and withdrawing support altogether. To view the war in such binary terms is not good for the United States. Nor is it good for Ukraine – or, at least, it puts Ukraine in the position of staking a huge gamble on the future evolution of US attitudes and politics.

Sadly, developing and debating alternatives has been difficult to impossible in a context of embedded idealism and exceptionalism in Washington, which has been reinforced by shock, fear and ingrained habits of dependence on America in most European capitals. Some of the more realistic approaches have been proposed by figures on the American right, whose views on other subjects are often problematic. On the American left, the universalism that animates progressives has made it hard for them to develop alternatives of their own.

There is obviously a strategic logic to punishing the Kremlin for its aggression, and we can continue to hope that Ukraine emerges from this conflict as a democracy with a bright European future. On the current course, however, we are in for a very long and very costly war over a relatively small amount of territory of limited strategic relevance to the United States. This essay does not offer in-depth proposals or plans to get off that course. But it does argue for ways in which both left and right should be striving for a more realistic approach to the war. Unless US policymakers can arrive at a constructively pragmatic realism, disaffected voters could revolt in a manner that exacerbates America's existing domestic political fractures.

The mainstream consensus

In the early days of the war, Russian forces demonstrated their incompetence to the world in their sloppy and ultimately failed effort to capture Kyiv. Meanwhile, Ukraine's political leadership – above all the brilliant performances of President Volodymyr Zelenskyy – demonstrated that it could sustain the national resolve to resist Russia's invasion. Seizing upon this pleasant surprise, the Washington foreign-policy establishment rapidly formed a consensus on what to do about Russia's aggression. The US government, major think tanks and several powerful media organisations united in calling for humanitarian, financial and especially military support for Kyiv, along with heavy sanctions on Russia in the name of defending Ukraine, democracy and the US-led world order. A week after the invasion, in his State of the Union address, President Joe Biden said that Russian President Vladimir Putin 'sought to shake the foundations of the free world', and that in response the United States would be 'inflicting pain on Russia and supporting the people of Ukraine'.[1] The *Washington Post*, in arguing that more weapons should be sent to Ukraine, stated in an editorial that 'Mr. Putin's war aim is not merely to conquer Ukraine but to overthrow the international order itself'.[2]

When the Ukrainians then fared surprisingly well against an initially disorganised and incompetent Russian force, more ambitious goals were proposed and adopted. Ukraine would not just escape the Russian onslaught with its sovereignty intact, it now needed to 'win' in order to punish Russia further and demonstrate the folly of Russia's invasion to the world.[3] Many of the emerging pro-war party in Washington also viewed Ukrainian victory as a moral imperative, although without any clear concept of what 'victory' entailed. A news cycle fixated on the drama of battles for specific towns and villages soon encouraged a narrowly operational, military narrative.[4] Neoconservative analysts who had authored the Iraq War experienced a revival, and put forward absolute military victory over Russia as the only logical policy.[5] Debates over broader strategic aims, policy trade-offs and alternative courses of action were muffled.

Calls for Ukrainian victory, still only vaguely defined, intensified after the revolting Russian massacre of Ukrainian civilians in Bucha was uncovered two months into the war, heightening the moral tenor of the debate.[6] As Representative Adam Schiff saw it, 'the war in Ukraine is a struggle of freedom against tyranny', and 'we must do our part to ensure Ukraine is victorious'.[7] Echoing the call was Nancy Pelosi, then speaker of the House of Representatives, who congratulated the Ukrainians on their 'outstanding defense of Democracy' and pledged to be with them 'until victory is won'.[8] After Ukraine's surprising and impressive advances in Kharkiv in September 2022, the push for an all-out Ukrainian victory grew even stronger. By the end of the year, it was a rallying call for a growing number of mainstream thinkers, even though the definition of what Ukrainian victory would mean in practice remained vague and varied. In this context, proposals for more calibrated US policy alternatives were sharply criticised, sometimes cast as treasonous. Even sincere and well-informed warnings of the threat of Russian nuclear use were treated as gullible sops for Kremlin propaganda. By early 2023, when Biden paid his dramatic visit to Kyiv and walked with Zelenskyy next to the city's gold-domed monastery of St Michael, it was clear that the United States had settled on a standing commitment.

March 2023 marked the 20th anniversary of the US invasion of Iraq. The occasion revived broad recrimination for the US entanglement there and the strategic tunnel vision that led to it. Iraq and Ukraine are distinguishable, but these historical reflections on the intellectual and cultural roots of that tragic phase in the history of US foreign policy seemed to take place in a separate universe from discussions about Ukraine policy.

The roots of the consensus

The consensus that underpinned US policy reflected the deep liberal-internationalist impulses of US foreign-policy elites and an abiding belief in American 'exceptionalism' and indispensability.[9] Many top US experts on Ukraine and NATO cut their teeth on the problems of post-Cold War Europe in the 1990s as ambassadors, National Security Council staff and military leaders. By virtue of their experience and seniority, this expert group has exerted outsize influence on US policy. For them, bringing Ukraine into the Western world has been not only an objective, but the denouement of a long quest that began with the Soviet retreat and was inspired by democratic-peace theory; aimed at building a Europe whole, free and at peace; and which America's extraordinary status of global hyperpower after the Cold War seemed to enable.

Also driving Washington's hawkish consensus on Ukraine policy was the pain of America's withdrawal from Afghanistan, which was still fresh. The withdrawal had infuriated many in the foreign-policy establishment and raised the spectre of future bouts of American retrenchment, thereby contributing to fears that a repressed American isolationism was soon to be loosed upon the world. Putin, for his part, may have taken the withdrawal as evidence that America would sit on the sidelines when he attacked Ukraine. If so, he gravely misread the room. For US policy elites, inaction in the face of Russia's attack would risk another blow to American prestige. Backing Ukraine, on the other hand, might revitalise America's self-image as a force for good in the world not only after Afghanistan, but after the unseemly Trump years and the global humiliation of the 6 January 2021 insurrection. This is not to deny the brutality of Russia's attack, or to claim that nothing should have been done to help Ukraine. But after Afghanistan, the COVID-19 pandemic and Trump, the United States was primed to overreact.

Ukraine's fight for freedom from Russian imperialism also struck a chord for many who feared America was in its own battle for democracy against internal foes. Freedom from imperialism and democratic freedom are not identical. Resisting imperial aggression – Russian or otherwise – may be praiseworthy, but it does not require being a democracy. In the Washington mentality, however, such nuance tends to be missed or ignored. Perhaps this is because America's own origin story conflates the two types of freedom. Perhaps it is because acknowledging the difference would weaken the case for Washington's deepening defence of Kyiv.

Either way, it is easy to underestimate the power that identifying the future of democracy with Ukraine's future has had in an America where anxiety about the country's own democracy is running near a fever pitch. On one level, there is the belief that the liberal world order is at stake – that if Putin is not stopped in Ukraine, democracy everywhere will be imperilled. Fortifying this belief are America's understanding of its role in stopping Nazi Germany in the Second World War – a mental schema easily if inaccurately analogised to aggressive military action against Russia now – and Ukraine's skilful portrayal of its self-defence as tantamount to the preservation of the universal values of freedom and democracy.

The defence of democracy in Ukraine also takes on a visceral character because Putin is the aggressor. Standing up to the man in the Kremlin conjures the valorous days of the Cold War. And Putin is especially repugnant to Democrats because he meddled in the 2016 US presidential elections, and because Trump kowtowed to him.[10] For some prominent Democrats, a line runs from far-right American militants' 6 January attack on the US Capitol to Russian tanks pointing their guns at Kyiv.[11] In likening arms for Ukraine to defending freedom itself, Biden appears to share this view.[12] It is a position that recalls George W. Bush's Manichaean post-9/11 foreign-policy rhetoric on Iraq and Afghanistan.

Critics on the right

Early on, powerful old-line Republican leaders such as senators Mitch McConnell, Roger Wicker and Jim Risch crossed the aisle to join the Democrats on the Ukraine consensus. They seemed keen to resurrect the foreign-policy pillars of the early Reagan administration, especially its stark ideological contrasts and high levels of military spending. In supporting the May 2022 aid package, Wicker noted that 'President Reagan once called the Soviet Union "the focus of evil in the modern world"', and argued that 'the Kremlin remains one of the chief forces for evil in our world'. 'Ukraine has become the front line in the contest between freedom and despotism', he said.[13] Other senior Republicans made similar connections early in the war, accepting the main tenets of the mainstream consensus and its Cold War-esque framing.[14]

Naturally, these traditionalists could not allow a Democratic administration to go unscathed, and so they positioned themselves on the hawkish side of the mainstream consensus, attacking the White House for holding back weapons from Ukraine and for failing to effectively monitor the weapons they had already sent. Even so, these senior Republicans faced a revolt within the party from its populist wing. This mostly younger, sometimes whacky group included representatives Matt Gaetz, Paul Gosar and

Marjorie Taylor Greene, as well as senators Josh Hawley and J.D. Vance. In the Republican-controlled House, opposition to Ukraine assistance packages grew from 54 members in March 2022 to 200 in September. Republican calls to rein in US support for Ukraine grew louder, reflecting declining support among Republican voters.[15] This led Representative Kevin McCarthy to proclaim that House Republicans would not write a 'blank check' for Ukraine under his leadership should Republicans win a majority in the midterm elections (as they did) and McCarthy become speaker (as he did).[16] When McCarthy was ejected from the leadership of an increasingly chaotic Republican House, his successor, Mike Johnson, proved to be if anything less willing to move a Ukraine aid package forward. As of early 2024 there is a possibility of a joint 'Ukraine–Israel–Taiwan' package, but no guarantee that it will pass.

In part, these Republican threats were predictable partisan attacks on Biden, but they were also rooted in deeper Republican philosophical and cultural currents. One was the long-standing libertarian critique of public spending of the kind once voiced by intellectuals such as Friedrich Hayek. Another was the nationalist strain in the Republican Party that prevailed before Dwight D. Eisenhower turned it towards liberal internationalism. Trump revived the nationalist views to some degree, but his foreign policy was so idiosyncratic that it also reflected the militant unilateralism espoused, for example, by John Bolton, his third national security advisor.

Populist Republican critiques of the mainstream consensus pointed to a more realistic approach to the conflict, but were mingled with unsavoury views on other issues. It was hard, for example, to divorce the populist arguments for strategic restraint from Trump's open admiration for Putin and his ridiculous claim, right before Russia invaded, that Putin was 'going to go in and be a peacekeeper'.[17] Trump had sometimes seemed so besotted with the Kremlin's strongman that he fuelled speculation that the Russian security services had collected *kompromat* on him during his time doing business deals in Moscow. It did not help that this flirtation was not limited to Trump. Other Republicans also warmed to the European far right – for instance, inviting Hungarian Prime Minister Viktor Orbán, who has proudly called himself illiberal, to speak at the 2022 Conservative Political Action Conference.

The Republican right's attack on the internationalist consensus was, moreover, sometimes tinged with a xenophobia that can bleed into the kind of racism that wiser conservatives have recognised as a pox on the party.[18] This was most evident in the peculiar linkage so many Republicans have drawn between the war in Ukraine and migration across the United States' southern border. It goes almost without saying that Trump made this connection early on, but many other Republicans echoed it over the course of 2022 and 2023, and it now features prominently in congressional negotiations over aid for Ukraine. Vance, for example, objected repeatedly to funding for Ukraine on the grounds that the real crisis was at the border, where there were allegedly 'more illegal drugs and more Democrat voters pouring into this country'.[19]

Republican critics have thus raised legitimate questions about the strategic importance of Ukraine, but they have too often done so in the service of a vision of America at odds with the multicultural nation that many others believe in and aspire to unite. This greatly weakens the appeal of their policy views.

Critics on the left

In the polarised political environment of the contemporary United States, the very fact that Republicans are doing the criticising probably drives the case among Democrats for unbridled support for Ukraine more than constraining it. This is also unhelpful to open debate and the proper calibration of US policy. The progressive left, however, did try to open space for debate, calling for a more robust diplomatic track. They failed miserably, but for very different reasons than the populists did.

Russia's invasion of Ukraine is essentially imperialist revanchism, which the American left has a long tradition of standing against. Usually American imperialism is the target, however. During the Cold War, the Soviet Union was very effective in hiding its imperialism and drawing attention to the West's. As a result, for progressives, some mental adjustment was needed in the face of Russia's attack. But as bodies piled up, the brutal face of Russian imperialism was hard to deny.

In the run-up to the war, progressives tended to emphasise the need for diplomacy and argue against lethal aid to Ukraine.[20] Some progressives voted nay to the first weapons authorisation, primarily out of concern that adding more weapons would only intensify the killing in a war that Ukraine seemed likely to lose anyway. Representative Ayanna Pressley, for example, argued that the money would 'only escalate the conflict, exacerbate the humanitarian crisis on the ground, and lead to an even larger catastrophe', adding that there was 'no military solution'.[21] Progressives like Representative Ilhan Omar also expected that broad-based sanctions, such as the ban on Russian oil passed in the early weeks of the war, would raise the war's humanitarian cost without significantly diminishing Putin's ability to wage it.[22]

As the war unfolded over the course of the spring, however, progressive thinking evolved.[23] Russian forces retreated from Kyiv and Ukraine seemed more likely to survive. Progressive support for sanctions and military assistance increased. After the Bucha massacre, all members of the 100-strong Congressional Progressive Caucus voted in favour of the unprecedented $40 billion May aid package. While they continued to stress the need for diplomacy, their advocacy was often maladroit. A 24 October 2022 letter released by the caucus largely backed the mainstream consensus, but also called for 'direct talks' between the United States and Russia aimed at ending the conflict. The document elicited vitriol. 'This letter is an olive branch to a war criminal who's losing his war', tweeted one fellow Democrat.[24] The caucus quickly withdrew and disavowed the letter, whose timing looked timorous in the face of Putin's recent annexations in eastern Ukraine, and nuclear bluster. Meanwhile Ukrainian advances in Kharkiv had raised false hope that Ukraine could win back more territory. The progressives' letter, moreover, seemed to align them against the White House and with the Republicans' threat to pull back US assistance from Kyiv. This was clearly not the signatories' intention, but it didn't matter, especially after the media's exaggerated portrayal of the letter as a call for the president to 'dramatically shift' policy.[25]

In any case, the episode showed how little space there was for reasoned discussion of alternatives to the mainstream consensus, and how costly it could be to challenge it. After the fallout, political contortion was predictable. Some progressives drew on the group's anti-imperialist traditions to argue that the United States needed to support Ukraine unconditionally, lest it impose quasi-imperial restraints on Kyiv.[26] But the reality remains far more complex. Providing Ukraine with weapons while abjuring the use of US leverage to encourage Kyiv to adopt realistic war aims is a recipe for protracted conflict. It works against the case for diplomacy and in fact runs counter to progressive traditions rooted in the social gospel and other principles of peace.

Part of the progressives' dilemma is that their intellectual tradition and culture is animated by a universalist idealism that has sat uncomfortably with foreign-policy realism that privileges US interests. This ostensible tension is arguably resolvable insofar as progressives' broader focus on domestic justice, race relations, economic inequality and corruption could anchor a foreign policy well attuned to the more pluralistic world that seems to be emerging, in which US hegemony has waned. It might also encourage a more sophisticated understanding of the strengths and weaknesses of American exceptionalism. Unfortunately, the debacle of the letter discouraged further efforts in this direction.

Risking strategic overreach

As the third year of the war looms, the mainstream consensus remains strong. The Biden administration has been wise to limit the weapons the United States provides to Ukraine and to proceed with restraint and seriousness about the risk of igniting a broader war. Background discussions with White House officials suggest glimmers of a more realistic policy on the horizon, but for the first two years of the war the administration has struggled to maintain that balance against hawkish voices, despite the fact that America's vital interests in Europe, including access to a large European economy and pool of like-minded democracies, have not been meaningfully damaged by the war or seriously threatened by Russian occupation of eastern Ukraine, however unjust.

What will happen in the third year of the war is uncertain, but the Ukraine debate has made it clear that the risk is not the dearth of American extroversion some feared before the war, but rather too much of it. It is unquestionably a good thing that the American foreign-policy debate has not descended into the depths of isolationism that many prominent foreign-policy experts have feared.[27] An internationally engaged America, ready to provide leadership when needed in the name of global peace and prosperity, is good for America and good for the world. But realism, diplomacy and restraint are essential components of any statecraft that is both strategic and open to a plural world order characterised by mutual coexistence. This is the kind of order that a wise foreign policy would strive to realise in a world where America is enormously powerful but no longer hegemonic; violence is pervasive; and the chance of cataclysmic great-power war and climactic and artificial-intelligence disasters loom large. But diplomacy and negotiations will require moderation of moral tone. It is hard to make the case for war against Putin on moral grounds and then restrict American military involvement. It is hard to claim that world order is at stake in a case like Ukraine and then exercise strategic restraint. Who is to say how much punishment must be meted out to Russia so that international order will be preserved?

Moderation of moral tone will unfortunately be very difficult as long as the foreign-policy establishment clings to lopsided historical tropes built on monocausal explanations of the war. Putin bears primary responsibility for the war and its killing. Russia's actions are clearly illegal under international law, as well as an outrage against human decency. But historians looking back on this tragedy years from now will find the origins of the war to be complex. It is a fantasy to pretend that the European Union's and NATO's promises to enlarge to Ukraine, and the growing Western military presence there, were not somehow part of that complexity. As long as American leaders insist that they are not, the Manichaean framing will endure, the US will fail to moderate its own moral tone, and American diplomats will be reduced to issuing stentorian moral injunctions rather than tackling the messy business of negotiation and compromise that is their real métier.

No one should pretend that the alternatives to fighting on would be easy or without risks and costs of their own. But in the constrained context of the debate in Washington, these alternatives have not been seriously considered or pursued. The multilateral efforts at peace that so many of the world's emerging powers have endorsed – albeit with varying degrees of seriousness – might, for example, have been leveraged more creatively. An indefinite ceasefire along the current lines of control would at least abate the violence and human suffering in Ukraine, as well as the war's worldwide economic consequences, even if it did not resolve the underlying political problems that led to the war in the first place. A ceasefire might include some type of commitment from the West to restart military assistance to Ukraine, potentially in greater force, if Russia attacked again. It might also include promises that Ukraine would lose Western support were it to restart the war itself, for example in an attempt to take Crimea by force. To be sure, this would be a tenuous peace, not unlike the peace that prevailed from 2014–22, and it might collapse just as that peace did. But it also might survive, and with luck, the underlying political problems would attenuate over time, even in the context of a cold hostility. Ukraine might then find the space to truly focus on post-conflict recovery, a process that already is likely to last decades and cost hundreds of billions, if not trillions, of euros. The prospect that it is overrun by Russia, which remains today, would be reduced.

One certain thing is that, after two years, continued war is not a path to resolving the political problems that brought this war on in the first place, and therefore, not a path to peace for the people of Ukraine or to the security of Europe.

* * *

The US foreign-policy establishment ought to consider how recurrent strategic overreach, which now looms also in the Middle East, could fuel even greater domestic American resentment against Washington. Dissenting positions on the left and right reflect the needs of underserved American communities – people who for reasons of race, economic exclusion or globalisation have been neglected in post-Cold War America's foreign and domestic policies. Progressives are clear about their preference for social and economic justice, the far right about its concern for deindustrialised white populations that Democrats have recently overlooked. Here are some fair points from Vance, for example:

> Bipartisan foreign policy consensus has led the country astray many times.
> Leadership in both parties supported the invasion of Iraq, the decades

long nation-building project in Afghanistan, regime change in Libya and guerrilla war in Syria. All of these policies cost a lot of money and killed many. None of those conflicts has served the nation's long-term interest.[28]

His argument is credible, though his views on other issues are so distasteful to liberals that it is almost impossible for them to credit him. But there are good reasons for liberals to listen a little more intently. The war in Ukraine could end in catastrophe or a costly stalemate; unalloyed Ukrainian victory is highly unlikely. Just as Trump capitalised on the unpopularity of the forever wars, the nationalist faction could win voters if they believed that the so-called liberal establishment had once again indulged in an expensive and vain adventure.

Rather than policing America's alleged isolationist cravings, America's deep bench of foreign-policy experts might focus more on illuminating concrete trade-offs that truly affect the American people. So far, the debate over Ukraine has shown how tough this is to do. But the United States has embraced pragmatic, judicious realism in the past, and should be able to do so again. In the case at hand, this would mean continuing a prudent level of support for Ukraine, but also evaluating the war through the lens of Ukraine's military, economic and political importance, rather than imagining that world order, democracy and freedom are at stake in every kilometre that is won or lost.

Notes

[1] White House, 'State of the Union Address', 1 March 2022, https://www.whitehouse.gov/state-of-the-union-2022/.

[2] 'Defeating Putin Will Require Larger U.S. Commitments – and Risks', *Washington Post*, 30 April 2022, https://www.washingtonpost.com/opinions/2022/04/30/defeating-vladimit-putin-ukraine-war-requires-larger-risks/.

[3] See, for example, Alina Polyakova and John Herbst, 'Ukraine Can Win: The Case Against Compromise', *Foreign Affairs*, 22 April 2022, https://www.foreignaffairs.com/articles/ukraine/2022-04-22/ukraine-can-win.

[4] See, for instance, Eliot A. Cohen, 'Don't Let Up Now', *Atlantic*, 28 March 2022, https://www.theatlantic.com/ideas/archive/2022/03/west-strategy-against-russia-ukraine-war/629387/.

[5] See *ibid*.

[6] See, for instance, 'The Bucha Massacre Marks Grim Turning Point in Russia's War', *Washington Post*, 4 April 2022,

https://www.washingtonpost.com/
opinions/2022/04/04/ukraine-bucha-
massacre-forceful-response/.

7 Adam Schiff (@RepAdamSchiff),
post to X, 1 May 2022, https://
twitter.com/RepAdamSchiff/
status/1520928506573688834.

8 Nancy Pelosi (@SpeakerPelosi),
post to X, 1 May 2022, https://
twitter.com/SpeakerPelosi/
status/1520672718823297032.

9 See Christopher S. Chivvis, 'The
Humility of Restraint: Niebuhr's
Insights for a More Grounded Twenty-
first-century American Foreign Policy',
Working Paper, Carnegie Endowment
for International Peace, November
2021, https://carnegieendowment.org/
files/Chivvis_Niebuhr_v2.pdf.

10 See Ivan Krastev, 'Why Are American
Liberals So Afraid of Russia?', New
York Times, 16 August 2017, https://
www.nytimes.com/2017/08/16/
opinion/american-liberals-vladimir-
putin-russia.html.

11 See Hillary Rodham Clinton and Dan
Schwerin, 'A State of Emergency for
Democracy', Atlantic, 25 February 2022,
https://www.theatlantic.com/ideas/
archive/2022/02/republicans-ukraine-
putin-xi-trump-democracy/622898/.

12 White House, 'Remarks by President
Biden on Continued Support for
Ukraine', 25 January 2023, https://
www.whitehouse.gov/briefing-
room/speeches-remarks/2023/01/25/
remarks-by-president-biden-on-
continued-support-for-ukraine/.

13 Senator Roger Wicker, 'Wicker Pushes
Military Aid for Ukraine', 2 May
2022, https://www.wicker.senate.
gov/2022/5/wicker-pushes-military-
aid-for-ukraine.

14 See, for example, Jim Risch, 'Guest
Opinion: Why Ukraine Matters', Idaho
Press, 20 March 2022, https://www.
idahopress.com/opinion/guest_opinions/
guest-opinion-why-ukraine-matters/
article_375378da-173e-5d22-8748-
219758a5fee7.html.

15 See Dina Smeltz, Craig Kafura and
Emily Sullivan, 'Growing US Divide on
How Long to Support Ukraine', Chicago
Council on Global Affairs, 5 December
2022, https://globalaffairs.org/research/
public-opinion-survey/growing-us-
divide-how-long-support-ukraine.

16 Quoted in Farnoush Amiri and Kevin
Freking, 'McCarthy: No "Blank Check"
for Ukraine if GOP Wins Majority', AP,
18 October 2022, https://apnews.com/
article/russia-ukraine-donald-trump-
humanitarian-assistance-congress-
c47a255738cd13576aa4d238ec076f4a.

17 Quoted in David Leonhardt, 'The
G.O.P.'s "Putin Wing"', New York
Times, 7 April 2022, https://www.
nytimes.com/2022/04/07/briefing/
republican-party-putin-wing.html.

18 See Ross Douthat, 'Can the Right
Escape Racism?', New York Times, 10
September 2019, https://www.nytimes.
com/2019/09/10/opinion/racism-
republicans-trump.html.

19 J.D. Vance (@JDVance1), post to X,
5 April 2022, https://twitter.com/
JDVance1/status/1511311385543815180.

20 See Congressional Progressive
Caucus, 'Congressional Progressive
Caucus Leaders Reps. Jayapal and
Lee Call for Diplomatic Solution to
Crisis in Ukraine', 26 January 2022,
https://progressives.house.gov/
press-releases?ID=DC95B5E6-BC94-
4DDC-812B-68AE063CC787; and
Ilhan Omar, 'Rep. Omar's Statement

on Proposed Ukraine Defense Bill', 2 February 2022, https://omar.house.gov/media/press-releases/rep-omars-state-ment-proposed-ukraine-defense-bill.

21 Ayanna Pressley, 'Rep. Pressley's Statement on Ukraine Votes', 10 March 2022, https://pressley.house.gov/2022/03/10/rep-pressley-s-state-ment-ukraine-votes/.

22 See Darragh Roche, 'Why Cori Bush and Ilhan Omar Joined Republicans in Voting Against Russia Oil Ban', *Newsweek*, 10 March 2022, https://www.newsweek.com/vote-against-russian-oil-ban-republicans-cori-bush-ilhan-omar-1686655.

23 See Matthew Duss, 'Why Ukraine Matters for the Left', *New Republic*, 1 June 2022, https://newrepublic.com/article/166649/ukraine-matters-american-progressives.

24 Jack Auchincloss (@JakeAuch), post to X, 24 October 2022, https://twitter.com/JakeAuch/status/1584727936816803842.

25 See, for instance, Yasmeen Abutaleb, 'Liberals Urge Biden to Rethink Ukraine Strategy', *Washington Post*, 24 October 2022 (updated 25 October 2022), https://www.washingtonpost.com/politics/2022/10/24/biden-ukraine-liberals.

26 See, for example, Jamie Raskin, 'Raskin Restates the Fundamental Importance of the Ukrainian Struggle for National Sovereignty, Democracy and Freedom', 25 October 2022, https://raskin.house.gov/press-releases?ID=C6AAEAAD-548C-444A-85AB-A77AB7FFAAE6.

27 Richard Haass, 'The Age of America First: Washington's Flawed New Foreign Policy Consensus', *Foreign Affairs*, 29 September 2021, https://www.foreignaffairs.com/articles/united-states/2021-09-29/biden-trump-age-america-first.

28 J.D. Vance, 'Trump's Best Foreign Policy? Not Starting Any Wars', *Wall Street Journal*, 31 January 2023, https://www.wsj.com/articles/trumps-best-foreign-policy-not-starting-any-wars-ukraine-russia-war-rocket-nuclear-power-weapons-defense-11675186959.

Ukraine's Fate and Europe's Future: A View from Sweden

Robert Dalsjö

Russia's war in Ukraine is not only about Ukraine's freedom and existence as an independent nation-state, or about human rights and freedom from oppression. At its heart, the war is about the future we are going to live in, about Europe and the European security order. Russian President Vladimir Putin has driven a tank through the common European house that Mikhail Gorbachev envisioned, brutally trampling the cooperative and democratic security order agreed upon in 1990. In its place, he wants to build a new order where might makes right, a tyranny whereby the big and strong do as they please and Russia is restored to what Putin presumes is its rightful place as an empire dominating at least half of Europe.

This yearning for empire is so powerful – and seemingly supported by so many Russians – that Moscow is prepared not only to lay waste to Ukraine in the process of achieving it, but also to sacrifice its own army and hundreds of thousands of its people, and to mortgage itself to China. By this evidence, Putin has gone all in, and cannot be talked into ending the war and returning to the status quo ante. He and Russia must be externally stopped, deterred and contained. If Russian aggression is not repelled in Ukraine, Moscow will be emboldened and in a strong position to threaten, coerce and generally cause trouble in the rest of Europe.

Robert Dalsjö is Director of Research at the Swedish Defence Research Agency. This article was adapted from a Survival Online blog post that was published in January 2024.

Survival | vol. 66 no. 1 | February–March 2024 | pp. 41–48   https://doi.org/10.1080/00396338.2024.2309072

How the war might end

There are three ways in which the war in Ukraine might end: a Russian victory, a Ukrainian victory or some kind of draw.

A Russian victory seemed unlikely after the failure of Russia's march on Kyiv and its 2022 summer offensive, followed by Ukrainian successes in the autumn.[1] But it seems more plausible after the failure of this past summer's Ukrainian offensive and clear signs of flagging Western support for Ukraine. Russia's main chance of winning this war rests on its willingness to keep fighting despite horrendous losses, and to wait for the West to grow tired and Ukraine to become exhausted. Delayed support packages in the European Union and the US Congress are encouraging to the Kremlin, as are the prospect of Donald Trump returning to power and mounting signs of division within Ukraine concerning the conduct of the war.

Russian victory would probably mean the annexation of much of Ukraine, with the rump state subservient to Moscow – much as Belarus is today – and the harsh suppression of Ukrainian nationality and human rights. Tens of millions of Ukrainians would flee to the safety of the EU. Feeling vindicated by victory, Putin would rebuild his forces, poise his armies on the Bug River and look to dominate half of Europe.

A Ukrainian victory, on the other hand, would seem to be contingent on Ukraine inflicting sufficient pain on Russia to trigger a military or political collapse. This looked likeliest in autumn 2022 in light of Ukraine's successful offensives, and then again in summer 2023 during Yevgeny Prigozhin's brief rebellion, but now seems a more distant possibility. Russia's defences in the south and east are holding, the Kremlin has managed to drum up more soldiers and more equipment, and the economy has been put on a war footing fuelled by oil exports. Domestic Russian dissent has been silenced and the general population remains passive or even apathetic.

The current situation seems closest to the third scenario: a draw or stalemate. Ukraine's Western-supported summer offensive having failed, General Valerii Zaluzhnyi, commander-in-chief of the Armed Forces of Ukraine, has acknowledged that the military conflict is deadlocked.[2] Defence is dominant, neither side can make headway in offensives even at an appalling cost in lives, and the war seems stuck in trench warfare reminiscent of the Western Front in 1914–18. Now, as then, it may come down to who can endure misery and death the longest.[3] Right now, Putin seems confident that Russia can outlast the West and exhaust Ukraine, forcing it to give up.

At some intermediate point, of course, both sides may need breathing space, negotiated or de facto. It would probably take the form of a temporary pause in the fighting while both sides rebuilt their forces to prepare for a new round. A stable and lasting peace whereby Ukraine would accept the loss of the occupied provinces seems impossible as long as the current regime remains in power in Moscow, as Putin would be apt to break any promises that contravened his imperial goal of erasing the state of Ukraine from the map, as he did in invading Ukraine in February 2022. What cannot be entirely ruled out, however, is something akin to the Korean Armistice Agreement, under which the Korean War is officially still on but little or no fighting takes place, despite perpetual tension and confrontation.[4]

Such a dispensation would come at the expense of Ukraine's territorial integrity, of the principle that territory should not be won by force and of the freedom of the people living in the occupied territories, which would be subjected to repression and Russification. The free part of Ukraine would have to be quickly admitted into NATO and the EU, much as the Federal Republic of Germany was in the 1950s, so as to establish a firm deterrent by way of security guarantees that would call for direct NATO action against Russia in the event of its breach of the agreement.[5]

State of play

Russia's war in Ukraine probably will not be over for years, and the West needs to prepare for a long haul. The West, of course, is far richer and more powerful than Russia. But Ukraine is highly dependent on outside military, political, financial and humanitarian support. The West's task is therefore to support Ukraine for long enough to dash Putin's hopes of outlasting Russia's adversaries. This will be materially demanding, but the cost pales in comparison to what Ukraine is paying in blood, destroyed lives and property, and national wealth. Moreover, the cost is a pittance next to that NATO would incur in fighting a war directly with Russia to defend NATO territory, which could materialise if Russia is not stopped now.[6]

Furthermore, if the West backs Ukraine only enough for it to avoid losing, but not enough for it to win, a stable and satisfactory result is unlikely. To muster the kind of full-blooded support that is required, the West will have to shed inhibitions about which weapons to provide, and urgently ramp up production of arms and ammunition. This does not mean transitioning to a wartime economy, as Russia has done, but rather easing restrictions, simplifying overcomplicated designs and bringing in new manufacturers.[7] The effort will not be wasted. Even after the war is over, whichever side wins, Russia will remain a long-term threat to Europe, and Europe will have to build a security order to contain Russia militarily, politically, economically and technologically.

Europe should be prepared to shoulder the lion's share of the post-war responsibility. It is our continent, our security and our future that are at stake. We are rich and can afford to protect ourselves. And even if US President Joe Biden should win the next election and keep America's isolationist forces at bay, the United States will still demand a more equitable sharing of burdens and will in the medium term have to shift its resources to meeting China's geopolitical challenge.

Sweden's evolving vocation

Like most European countries, Sweden believed that the threat of major war had ended in 1990, and dipped heavily into the peace dividend, reducing its once-large military to a small force geared for international peace operations. Despite clear warnings – Putin's Wehrkunde speech and the suspension of the Treaty on Conventional Armed Forces in Europe in 2007, the invasion of Georgia in 2008, the annexation of Crimea and the war in Donbas in 2014 – Sweden was unprepared for Russia's full-scale attack on Ukraine. Sweden then found itself with a considerable security deficit, or deterrence deficit as I have called it.[8] Its peacetime attempts to offset that strategic shortfall by cultivating bilateral ties with NATO members proved grossly inadequate, as the political and military situation made it brutally clear that NATO security guarantees could realistically apply only to members. Sweden's decision to join NATO resulted from the shock effect of Russia's invasion of Ukraine, the Social Democrats' strong party discipline, the centre-right opposition parties' standing support for NATO membership and, not least, Sweden's traditionally strong ties with Finland.

Finland was once an integral part of Sweden, and the two countries have remained close. But Finland's exposed geopolitical position, its 1939–40 Winter War against Soviet invasion and its semi-soft post-Second World War co-optation by the Soviet Union – grimly canonised as 'Finlandisation' – have produced a very different mindset. Finland's hard fate has forced it to be a nation of realists, and it joined NATO out of a sense of imminent danger, driven by its tragic history and, notably, public opinion. Sweden, with its charmed modern history and shielded geographic position, could afford to be more idealistic. To a significant degree, it applied for NATO membership out of a sense of moral outrage, but Sweden also felt compelled to follow Finland, despite the Swedish government having categorically ruled out NATO membership at a party conference just six months earlier. If Sweden had remained non-aligned, it would have constituted a barrier between Finland and its NATO allies, a politically painful and probably untenable position.[9] And Sweden's support for Ukraine against Russia runs deep in the population, political parties, press and government. Politically jarring as the shift may be, idealism informs hard-nosed policy. Sweden's challenge is to make it work.

Sweden's NATO challenge

Sweden is busy preparing to become a full NATO ally and to share the Alliance's burden of deterring Russia. The mental challenge alone is considerable: learning to think as an ally as opposed to a solitary actor; seeing solidarity in terms of commitments of resources rather than grand pronouncements; and fully embracing deterrence, including nuclear deterrence. Swedes will have to become team players rather than backseat drivers. But this adjustment will have to occur while Sweden undertakes three other urgent tasks: readying the armed forces for warfare, expanding the army, and adapting its military capabilities to Alliance operations.

The readiness imperative applies to all three services, but most emphatically to the army, which faces similar problems to those of the German army, including too many unfilled positions; shortages of equipment, ammunition, consumables and spare parts; and inadequate training, especially at higher levels of command. Politically as well as practically, realising the NATO-mandated capacity to field two forward-deployed brigades within ten to 30 days – whether by requiring conscripts to serve abroad or by hiring many more contract soldiers – will be difficult. In addition, doubling the size of the army from two to four brigades may exceed Sweden's ability in the short term, especially after having donated so much equipment to Ukraine.

While the army will be performing basically the same tasks as before, the naval and air services will have to take on new tasks and capabilities. The air force will need to discard its focus on defensive counter-air and naval strike in favour of ground attack, long-range precision strike and suppression of enemy air defences. The navy, for its part, will have to shift from being a 'light' navy whose primary mission is to repel a Russian seaborne invasion close to shore to a heavier force that enhances NATO's sea-control mission by maintaining maritime superiority in the Baltic Sea and securing sea lines of communication to Finland, the Baltics and Poland. This will mean abandoning long-held dispositions and doctrine, as well as acquiring new types of weapons and more capable ships suited for the open sea.[10]

*   *   *

For a while, many if not most Westerners thought major wars in Europe were a thing of the past, that humanity had turned a corner, and that the future was bright and peaceful. It seemed that Russia, and even China, would become more like Western nations and could be welcomed into that family. But the 25 years that followed the fall of the Berlin Wall turned out to be a holiday from history, now decidedly over. Russia has emerged as a predatory power that considers itself an enemy of the West and the European project, seeking revenge and the return of empire.

There is an understandable tendency to make Putin the prime culprit, but the problem runs deeper and transcends political personalities. Europe has a Russia problem writ large. Despite Europe's efforts to integrate Russia, it has displayed a nineteenth-century political disposition, believing it has a natural right to rule over its smaller neighbours and to dominate much of

Europe. This attitude is structural and likely to persist, to varying degrees, long after Putin has left the Kremlin.[11]

Empires, of course, seldom crumble or fall without turbulence or bloodshed, and the problems we are now facing can be seen as delayed effects of the fall of the Soviet empire. Arguably, it is lucky that this problem is arising at this moment rather than in the 1990s, as the states of Eastern Europe are now largely politically stable, self-sufficient and integrated into the EU and NATO. This observation, however, is not likely to console the Ukrainians. Should Russia win the ongoing war outright, it would be apt to conclude that it had defeated a weak and divided West. Deterrence in Europe would be severely weakened and, with America turning to face China, Europe might well emerge more vulnerable than it has been since the Second World War.

In Europe as in Sweden, idealism and practical compulsion have converged. The 'Europe whole and free' envisaged by George H.W. Bush in 1989, less than six months before the Berlin Wall fell, has not yet been won.[12] To secure it, the West must decisively turn back Russia's assault on Europe's peaceful and democratic order by helping Ukrainians preserve their nation substantially intact.

Notes

1 See Robert Dalsjö, Michael Jonsson and Johan Norberg, 'A Brutal Examination: Russian Military Capability in Light of the Ukraine War', *Survival*, vol. 64, no. 3, June–July 2022, pp. 7–28.

2 See 'Ukraine's Commander-in-chief on the Breakthrough He Needs to Beat Russia', *The Economist*, 1 November 2023, https://www.economist.com/europe/2023/11/01/ukraines-commander-in-chief-on-the-breakthrough-he-needs-to-beat-russia.

3 See Franz-Stefan Gady and Michael Kofman, 'Ukraine's Strategy of Attrition', *Survival*, vol. 65, no. 2, April–May 2023, pp. 7–22; and

Michael Jonsson and Johan Norberg, 'Russia's War Against Ukraine: Military Scenarios and Outcomes', *Survival*, vol. 64, no. 6, December 2022–January 2023, pp. 91–122.

4 See, for example, Carter Malkasian, 'The Korea Model: Why an Armistice Offers the Best Hope for Peace in Ukraine', *Foreign Affairs*, vol. 103, no. 4, July/August 2023, pp. 36–51; and Sergey Radchenko, 'This War May Be Heading for a Cease-fire', *New York Times*, 24 February 2023, https://www.nytimes.com/2023/02/24/opinion/ukraine-russia-war-korea.html.

5 See François Heisbourg, 'How to End a War: Some Historical Lessons

for Ukraine', *Survival*, vol. 65, no. 4, August–September 2023, pp. 7–24.

6   For a plausible way forward, see, in this issue of *Survival*, Franz Stefan-Gady and Michael Kofman, 'Making Attrition Work: A Viable Theory of Victory for Ukraine', *Survival*, vol. 66, no. 1, February–March 2024, pp. 7–24.

7   See Hannah Aries, Bastian Giegerich and Tim Lawrenson, 'The Guns of Europe: Defence-industrial Challenges in a Time of War', *Survival*, vol. 65, no. 3, June–July 2023, pp. 7–24.

8   See Robert Dalsjö, 'Sweden and its Deterrence Deficit: Quick to React, Yet Slow to Act', in Nora Vanaga and Toms Rostoks (eds), *Deterring Russia in Europe: Defence Strategies for Neighbouring States* (London: Routledge, 2018).

9   The Swedish foreign minister at the time reportedly said: 'Damn Finland, now we might have to join too.' See Maggie Strömberg and Torbjörn Nilsson, 'Så gick det till när S vände om Nato' [This is what happened when the Social Democrats turned around on NATO], *Svenska Dagbladet*, 2 July 2022, https://www.svd.se/a/Qy1gXx/sa-gick-det-till-nar-magdalena-andersson-kovande-om-nato.

10   On Sweden's transition into NATO, see Viltaute Zarembaite, Christopher Skaluba and Ann Marie Dailey, 'Navigating Sweden's NATO Membership: Insights for Political and Operational Adaptation', Issue Brief, Atlantic Council, 22 December 2023, https://www.atlanticcouncil.org/in-depth-research-reports/issue-brief/navigating-swedens-nato-membership-insights-for-political-and-operational-adaptation/.

11   See, for example, Thomas Graham, *Getting Russia Right* (Cambridge: Polity, 2023).

12   US Diplomatic Mission to Germany, 'A Europe Whole and Free', remarks to the citizens of Mainz, Federal Republic of Germany, by George Bush, 31 May 1989, https://usa.usembassy.de/etexts/ga6-890531.htm.

Argentina's Foreign Policy Under Milei: Limited Disruption?

Irene Mia

Javier Milei's decisive win in the run-off of Argentina's presidential elections in November 2023 confirmed a pattern of anti-incumbent voting in Latin America. His victory underscored rising popular dissatisfaction with decades of Peronist rule and signalled a strong desire for radical shifts in domestic policies amid a worsening socio-economic crisis. Milei, an ultra-libertarian economist with limited political experience, campaigned on a disruptive platform, advocating substantial reductions in the state's role in the economy, the adoption of dollarisation and the abolition of the central bank. This agenda aimed to tackle long-standing macroeconomic imbalances and stimulate economic activity to counter persistent economic stagnation, increasing poverty rates, triple-digit inflation, high levels of debt and negative net foreign reserves.[1]

Milei's rhetoric also telegraphed significant changes in Argentina's foreign policy and external relations. The top lines were a geopolitical reorientation towards the West and a departure from the Global South's agendas and associated forums, such as BRICS. The latter would supposedly involve cutting links with 'communist' countries such as Brazil and China, Argentina's largest trading and economic partners. It would also de-prioritise Argentina's involvement in Mercosur, South America's regional trade-integration project and putatively a central pillar of the country's trade policy and multilateral economic diplomacy, initially established by Brazil, Paraguay, Uruguay and Argentina itself in 1991.[2]

Irene Mia is an IISS Senior Fellow and Editor of the *Armed Conflict Survey*.

Survival | vol. 66 no. 1 | February–March 2024 | pp. 49–56   https://doi.org/10.1080/00396338.2024.2309073

Milei has resolutely initiated shock therapy for the domestic economy.[3] But he has proceeded more cautiously on the foreign-policy front, moderating some of his earlier broadsides against China and Brazil and his reservations about Mercosur. The political imperative of stabilising the domestic situation in the context of a fragmented Congress and powerful labour unions is likely to constrain changes in foreign policy, at least in the short to medium term. Furthermore, Milei's commitment to free trade and a minimal state is liable to make him hesitant to intervene extensively in trade and economic relations.

Geopolitical ambition vs economic reality

At the core of Milei's vision of foreign policy is the concept of Argentina as a capitalist and culturally 'Western' nation that should be aligned with the United States and developed market economies. This rationale explains the confrontational tone towards so-called communist countries – China especially, but also Brazil under the centre-left administration of Luiz Inácio 'Lula' da Silva – and limited interest in aligning with or championing some of the Global South's pivotal objectives. These include a more representative global order and a reformed global financial architecture. Milei's Western orientation also informs his lack of enthusiasm for revitalising Mercosur or joining BRICS.

For Milei, the Paris-based Organisation for Economic Co-operation and Development, rather than BRICS, should be Argentina's North Star. The proposed dollarisation of the Argentinian economy sharply contrasts with BRICS countries' enduring efforts to de-dollarise the global financial system.[4] Also illustrative is Milei's unwavering support for Israel, as part of the 'free world', and Ukraine.[5] This stance distinguishes him from other Latin American and Global South leaders, who have displayed ambivalence on both issues.[6]

Yet, while Argentina may be culturally close to the West, it is increasingly dependent on China for trade, investment and credit lines, including currency swaps, which have often proven to be a lifeline for Argentina.[7] Argentina joined China's Belt and Road Initiative in February 2022 and was one of six nations invited to join the BRICS bloc in August 2023. Brazil continues to be Argentina's largest trading partner, and Mercosur represents its best opportunity to secure privileged access to the desirable European Union market through an association agreement between the two blocs long in development.[8] In the short term, ties with China, Brazil and Mercosur are essential to Argentina's socio-economic stability. They would also facilitate Milei's longer-term economic agenda, including dollarisation and economic liberalisation and privatisation.

Privatisation and further liberalisation of key sectors such as energy and commodities are likely to produce substantial investment opportunities.[9] At the same time, the need to reactivate the economy quickly will prevent Milei's government from being overly selective about investors or deterring them with ad hoc bans or regulations based on nationality. Such an approach would also contradict Milei's free-market principles and deregulation agenda, and introduce uncertainty about the rules of the game. On balance, therefore, Chinese investors with deep pockets, a relatively low aversion to risk and a well-established presence in the country will inevitably continue to play a crucial role in Argentina's future. Should Milei persist in his climate-change denialism, moreover, he is likely to discourage environmentally and socially conscious investors in Europe and America from doing business in Argentina, effectively improving China's position.

Mercosur holds the most potential for Argentina's efforts to diversify markets and investment sources. The country's negotiating position vis-à-vis other regions (including the West) is stronger when it is part of a cohesive trade group – which also ensures preferential access to the vast Brazil market – than alone. Intra-Mercosur trade is also key to Argentina's effort to diversify away from commodities to higher-value-added goods.

Overall continuity

As Milei's victory appeared more likely, he seemed to grow more cognisant of the myriad constraints he would confront in restructuring Argentina's foreign and trade policies to align with his ideological inclinations and initial campaign pledges. During the first month of his tenure, he encountered formidable obstacles to initiating radical domestic reforms.

The Confederación General del Trabajo (CGT) – the most powerful trade union in the country, allied to the Peronists – swiftly lodged a legal challenge to the labour-reform provisions of Milei's comprehensive deregulation decree of 20 December; the court found them unconstitutional and partially suspended the decree. In response to the legislative package he sent to Congress, the CGT called a general strike on 24 January – early in a president's term even by Argentinian standards. The decree and legislative package face significant challenges in Congress. Milei's La Libertad Avanza party holds a meagre 39 (out of 257) seats in the lower chamber and eight (out of 72) in the Senate. Even with the backing of former president Mauricio Macri's Propuesta Republicana, majority support is unlikely unless La Libertad Avanza gains support from Peronist legislators, particularly in the Senate.[10] The broad scope of both measures – which grant the president the power to legislate by decree for an initial two-year period, extendable for another two years until the end of his term – and Milei's failure to consult with potential allies have raised concerns about excessive executive power. These reactions underscored the advisability of maintaining serviceable relations with existing trade and economic partners – crucial sources of potential investment and foreign reserves.

Accordingly, Milei's administration started mending relations with Lula and stopped talks of leaving Mercosur, instead expressing a keen interest in constructing a 'larger, enhanced Mercosur'.[11] It also expressed satisfaction with the existing state of the EU–Mercosur association agreement, aligning with Lula and withdrawing prior Argentine reservations about signing the agreement in its present form.[12] This unexpected convergence between Argentina and Brazil could generate fresh momentum towards finalising the agreement, at least from the Mercosur side. And Milei's embrace of Mercosur may prove game-changing for the bloc's future evolution. Although initially envisioned as a mechanism for member countries to enhance their integration into the global economy, Mercosur's external outreach has stagnated for years due to political differences among its members regarding the pace and scope of liberalisation. Argentina and Brazil's reinvigorated involvement would enable the group to negotiate agreements with other countries or regions from a more robust collective position, with the added benefit of alleviating internal tensions over the pace of liberalisation, heightened by Uruguay's efforts to negotiate trade deals on its own.[13]

Milei has also taken a more conciliatory tone with China, exchanging cordial letters with Chinese President Xi Jinping.[14] Statements stressing that Argentina would not sever ties with China and is committed to bilaterally supporting private-sector trade imply Milei's pragmatic acknowledgement that, in view of Argentina's heavy economic reliance on China, attempting to change the status quo wholesale would be rash. To be sure, Milei has endeavoured to distance his country from China somewhat. For instance, his administration secured a $960 million bridge loan from CAF – Development Bank of Latin America and the Caribbean – to fulfil its scheduled payment to the IMF in December, obviating the need to access a currency-swap line that China was preparing to offer.[15] Argentina also turned down the invitation to join the BRICS grouping, but it expressed its refusal politely, characterising the current moment as not 'opportune' for full membership while registering a commitment to improved relations, as well as increased trade and investment with the bloc's members.

*   *   *

Milei's vision of Argentina as a Western power aligned with the prevailing global order and financial system chafes against the economic reality of a country grappling with a severe economic crisis that is deeply dependent on China and Brazil for its economic sustainability. His call for significant broadening of economic and political ties with the United States also appears unrealistic. The US has committed to supporting him on economic reform and offered assistance in developing Argentina's upstream lithium industry.[16] But it lacks the economic capacity to replace China as the primary external actor in Argentina's economy. Furthermore, Milei's political beliefs, beginning with his scepticism about climate change, are likely to create friction with the present US Democratic administration. If he does not moderate them, American as well as EU investment in Argentina stands to decline, and tensions could arise over the United States' and the EU's extra-territorial application of environmental, social and governance regulations. Donald Trump's return to power, should it come to pass, might yield closer relations between the two countries. But even that would not substantially elevate Argentina's importance in US foreign policy.

Notes

1   See, for example, George Glover, 'This Is the World's Next Major Election. The Winner Has to Fix Chronic Hyperinflation and Halt a 6th Recession in 10 Years', *Business Insider*, 11 November 2023, https:// www.businessinsider.com/economy-argentina-hyperinflation-drought-rolling-recession-dedollarization-javier-milei-peso-2023-11?r=US&IR=T.

2   See Council on Foreign Relations, 'Mercosur: South America's Fractious Trade Bloc', last updated 18 December 2023, https://www.cfr.org/backgrounder/mercosur-south-americas-fractious-trade-bloc.

3   Milei followed up his sombre 'there's no money' inauguration speech with a whopping 54% peso devaluation and a barrage of measures – including major cuts to Argentina's traditionally generous fuel and transport subsidies, a reduction of the number of ministers from 18 to nine, discretionary transfers to the provinces, and a suspension of all new public construction projects and state advertising – aimed at producing savings equivalent to around 3% of GDP and moving closer to the stated zero-deficit goal by the end of 2024. He also announced tax increases on imported and exported goods. At the same time, the president moved swiftly on economic liberalisation and privatisation with a sweeping decree scrapping more than 350 regulations due to take effect before the end of 2023, though parts related to labour-market liberalisation have since been frozen by courts. He also sent an ambitious legislative package to Congress, asking it to reform the country's tax system, electoral law and public-debt management, and to authorise the privatisation of more than 40 state companies on an expedited basis. See Lucinda Elliott and Jorgelina Do Rosario, 'Explainer: What Is in Javier Milei's Sweeping Argentina Reform Bill?', Reuters, 29 December 2023, https://www.reuters.com/world/americas/what-is-javier-mileis-sweeping-argentina-reform-bill-2023-12-28/; and 'Javier Milei Implements Shock Therapy in Argentina', *The Economist*, 13 December 2023, https://www.economist.com/the-americas/2023/12/13/javier-milei-implements-shock-therapy-in-argentina.

4   See ISPI, 'A BRICS+ Challenge to the Dollar?', 7 September 2023, https://www.ispionline.it/en/publication/a-brics-challenge-to-the-dollar-139933.

5   Ukrainian President Volodymyr Zelenskyy attended Milei's inauguration ceremony in Buenos Aires – his first trip to Latin America – to thank him for his support. Milei also offered to organise a summit with Latin American and Ukrainian representations. See 'Ukraine's Zelenskyy Visits Argentina in Bid to Win Support from Global South', Voice of America, 10 December 2023, https://www.voanews.com/a/ukraine-s-zelenskyy-visits-argentina-in-bid-to-win-support-from-global-south/7392116.html.

6   See 'Russia's Pockets of Support Are Growing in the Developing World',

Economist Intelligence Unit, 7 March 2023, https://www.eiu.com/n/russias-pockets-of-support-are-growing-in-the-developing-world/.

7   See 'China Activates $6.5 Bln Swap Line with Argentina', Reuters, 18 October 2023, https://www.reuters.com/markets/currencies/china-clears-65-bln-part-argentina-swap-line-deal-2023-10-18/.

8   For an analysis on the importance of trade with Brazil and Mercosur, see Max Klaver, 'What Milei Means for Mercosur', Foreign Policy, 18 December 2023, https://foreignpolicy.com/2023/12/18/milei-mercosur-argentina-economy-trade/.

9   Industries include lithium, a critical mineral for the energy transition for which Argentina accounts for around 6% of global reserves and 20% of global production. See Juan Pablo Medina Bickel and Irene Mia, 'Geopolitics and Climate Change: The Significance of South America', Survival, vol. 65, no. 4, August–September 2023, pp. 123–38.

10   See, for instance, Michael Stott, 'Argentina's Milei Faces Enormous Hurdles to Govern', Financial Times, 20 November 2023, https://www.ft.com/content/fc2a1b7d-885c-49d4-bdd7-fc2463df405b.

11   'Mondino aseguró que Milei respaldará el acuerdo entre el Mercosur y la Unión Europea', Ámbito, 26 November 2023, https://www.ambito.com/economia/mondino-aseguro-que-milei-respaldara-el-acuerdo-el-mercosur-y-la-union-europea-n5885101.

12   See 'Argentina's Outgoing Government Rejects EU–Mercosur Trade Deal, but Incoming Administration Backs It', AP News, 4 December 2023, https://apnews.com/article/argentina-eu-mercosur-brazil-paraguay-7448623940e803b314ccd021f22ad7da.

13   See 'Uruguay, a Failed Mercosur Summit and China's Long Shadow', MercoPress, 30 December 2022, https://en.mercopress.com/2022/12/30/uruguay-a-failed-mercosur-summit-and-china-s-long-shadow.

14   See Natalie Liu, 'Argentina Not Joining BRICS Despite Xi's Personal Letter to Milei', Voice of America, 1 December 2023, https://www.voanews.com/a/argentina-not-joining-brics-despite-xi-s-personal-letter-to-milei/7380722.html.

15   See Facundo Iglesia, 'CAF Approves US$1 Billion Loan to Argentina with IMF Support', Buenos Aires Herald, 15 December 2023, https://buenosairesherald.com/economics/caf-approves-us1-billion-loan-to-argentina-with-imf-support.

16   See Adam Jourdan, 'U.S. Offers Argentina's Milei Support on IMF, Lithium, White House Adviser Says', Reuters, 10 December 2023, https://www.reuters.com/world/americas/us-offers-argentinas-milei-support-imf-lithium-white-house-adviser-2023-12-10/.

From Quad to Quint? Vietnam's Strategic Potential

James Adams, David C. Gompert and Thomas Knudson

Of all the world problems vying for American attention and resources, few are as profound as securing the world's most strategically important region, East Asia, from China's attempt to make it an exclusive sphere of influence. Even with Australia, India, Japan and the United States configured as the Quadrilateral Security Dialogue, known as the 'Quad', meeting this challenge with military power alone is becoming more difficult and perilous as Chinese military capabilities grow. At best, it will take years for the US military to end its reliance on the concentration of aircraft carriers and air bases in the Western Pacific that are within range of Chinese weapons and therefore vulnerable.[1]

A larger concept is needed, one that forges and employs economic power alongside military power, recalling the role that European economic integration and vitality played in tandem with NATO's military strength in containing the Soviet Union. Such a concept could exploit China's stumbling economy and trade dependence on the very nations that seek to constrain it. Here Vietnam could be pivotal. Turning it into a military adversary of China is not desirable, necessary or feasible, and it is the Vietnamese people who should and will determine their country's disposition towards their northern neighbour. But Vietnam can still become a sturdy partner of the United States as a means of achieving its own goals. Notwithstanding the long, dark spectre of the Vietnam War, in one 2017 poll, over 80% of Vietnamese

James Adams is former Vice President for Asia at the World Bank. **David C. Gompert** is former US Acting Director of National Intelligence. **Thomas Knudson** is former Chairman of the US Business Council for Sustainable Development.

Survival | vol. 66 no. 1 | February–March 2024 | pp. 57–65   https://doi.org/10.1080/00396338.2024.2309074

adults had a favourable view of the United States; only 6% had an unfavourable view.[2] Nearly 80% of Vietnamese distrust China, substantially higher than the regional average.[3]

Vietnam's potential

Vietnam lies at a global intersection. It has a 3,200-kilometre coastline mostly on the South China Sea, which hosts half the world's fishing, half the world's tanker- and merchant-fleet traffic, 20% of all world trade and vast fossil reserves.[4] Vietnam also has a 1,300 km border with China. And it is a cog of the Association of Southeast Asian Nations (ASEAN), which is one of the largest trading partners of the United States, the European Union and China.

Just as important as geography is the legendary work ethic of the Vietnamese people, who number 100 million. To spotlight Vietnam's cheap labour is to ignore its innate dynamism. A predicate of this dynamism is the native optimism of the Vietnamese.[5] Vietnam's economy is one of the world's fastest growing – 6% annually over 20 years – propelled increasingly by manufacturing exports. It is becoming a hub for microelectronic devices owing to accelerating foreign direct investment (FDI). Since the United States diplomatically recognised Vietnam in 1995, private-sector trade has grown astoundingly. Vietnamese exports to the United States totalled $127.5 billion in 2022.[6]

Sustaining such exceptional growth is not assured. Vietnam must shift from reliance on low-cost labour to high worker productivity if it is to emerge as a middle-income nation and true partner of the United States, Japan and other major powers. If it does not, its low-cost advantage could become self-perpetuating and self-defeating – a trap the Vietnamese are determined to avoid. Internationally, Vietnam's location and prospective productivity imply potential geo-economic influence in and beyond the region by virtue of sustained growth, competitiveness, raised living standards and exemplary development. With further impetus, these assets can contribute to prosperity and political stability throughout Southeast Asia, as the South Korean and Japanese economies have done for decades in Northeast Asia.

While Vietnam's eventual democratisation would help, it is not assured. Nor is it an immediate prerequisite for advancing the country's geo-economic influence. For now, the state is an agent for economic reforms, and it is investing heavily in education and training in order to build human capital.

Vietnam's new-found geo-economic vitality suggests a formula for recasting the US-led grand strategy to prevent China from expanding its regional control. Because China has failed to make political inroads with its Asian neighbours and is struggling financially and demographically, it is more susceptible to broad-gauged containment than it is to military balancing alone. Of late, the growth in China's military spending (about 7%) has exceeded that of its GDP (about 4%).[7]

Vietnam's goals

The Vietnamese state and people seek to end poverty, become a middle-income nation, protect the environment and neutralise Chinese threats. These goals dovetail with its potential as a development model and partner that is competitive in global trade and can become a reliable alternative source of advanced manufacturing. After successive (and successful) wars with France, the United States and China for independence and unification, the Vietnamese have chosen to pursue these aims without relying on military might. Vietnam spends just 2% of its GDP on defence, though the proportion is now growing because of China. Instead of massing defensive forces along the frontier with China, Vietnam has prioritised maritime security and cyber defence with Chinese mischief in mind.

The core challenge facing Vietnam is not to defend against Chinese aggression but to embark on lasting growth by improving per worker productivity, reinvigorating development and joining apt partnerships. The United States is not alone in expanding economic ties with Vietnam. India's trade with Vietnam is growing by over 20% annually; Australia's grew by more than 60% from 2021 to 2022; and Japan–Vietnam trade is nearly $50bn per annum. Surging FDI in Vietnam from these countries reflects both their intent to develop alternative supply chains and Hanoi's intent to depend less on China.[8]

America's interests

The Quad is unabashedly designed to oppose China's attempts to expand its control. Each member brings significant military strength to the partnership for bolstering deterrence and, if necessary, repelling Chinese aggression

– for instance, against Taiwan. China's complaint that the Quad aims to encircle it is not inaccurate. But stability through military strength alone is precarious. How long will it take the United States to mitigate the growing vulnerability of its forces in the Western Pacific? What if India and China resolve their Himalayan dispute? Could growing Japanese military power upset the regional balance? Might incidents involving military or intelligence units touch off escalation? What if deterrence fails and a massive war ensues? Can the United States maintain military superiority in the Western Pacific given Russian and Iranian threats elsewhere?

Both the size and character of the Quad could be stretched. In light of Vietnam's deepening ties with current members, it is a strong candidate to join a de facto 'Quint'. The United States can take the lead in encouraging this eventuality by aligning its policies with Vietnam's goal of reinvigorated development. Building up Vietnam's military and offering it a defence treaty would ignore Vietnam's own preferences, trigger a Chinese reaction and unsettle Southeast Asia.

With a containment strategy that leavens military power with economic power, a Quint can more easily confront China without military escalation. At the same time, some coercive advantages do arise from economic asymmetry. Waging economic warfare with China would, of course, damage the world economy, including the economies of the combatants. Still, it is important to impress upon China the scale of its vulnerability. As of 2021, Chinese exports to Australia, India, Japan, the United States and Vietnam exceeded $1 trillion per annum, or roughly one-fifth of China's per capita income. Chinese imports from those countries are roughly half that.[9] While there are other factors germane to economic conflict – for instance, China's large holdings of dollar-denominated securities – the sheer shock of lost revenue and jobs from ruptured trade would hit China dramatically, disproportionately and with unpredictable political effects.

Two cases

The strategy suggested here would bolster deterrence in two critical contexts: a Chinese attempt to take Taiwan by force or duress, and China's unrelenting efforts to gain effective control over most of the vital South China Sea.

An outright Chinese military assault with intent to occupy Taiwan is among the least plausible scenarios, as it would likely lead to full-scale war with the United States, Japan and Australia at least, opening up military opportunities for India in the Himalayas. The effects of economic warfare would pale in comparison to the destructiveness of kinetic and cyber warfare, and thus add little to deterrence. However, in more likely scenarios involving China's intimidation of Taiwan short of military attack, the prospect of an economic reaction by the Quad (or Quint) could afford the United States and its partners a form of escalation dominance. If China is deterred from military actions that could result in hostilities, it would also find itself at a disadvantage in terms of economic leverage during a crisis.

The economic clout of a cohesive US partnership could work to diminish disputes, quell Chinese aggression and reduce the potential for hostilities in the South China Sea. Despite the complexity of claims and counterclaims in these waters, one outcome favoured by most of the littoral states other than China – especially Vietnam – is a code of conduct. Vietnam's prospective partners could enhance the enforceability of such a code. Australia, Japan, India and the United States all have major equities in South China Sea security and in international freedom of navigation. A coalition including those powers alongside Vietnam and other ASEAN nations would raise the cost of aggressive Chinese unilateralism.

US economic strategy

After a generation of mostly just talk since the 1992 Rio Conference on Environment and Development, it is high time for focused progress.[10] FDI and trade are useful, of course, but because Vietnam is neither undeveloped nor fully developed and has a dynamic economy, it would make an ideal proof of concept for a new US-led world-development campaign. To this end, well-targeted US private–public initiatives could help Vietnam re-energise growth through productivity and renewable development.

Vietnam could be a pathfinder for renewable development, which optimises production outputs and inputs across sectors, conserves water and energy, guides infrastructure build-out and protects the environment.[11] In economic development as in nature itself, there need be no such thing as waste. Through co-location of industry and optimisation of infrastructure, producers' by-products can serve as others' inputs. Properly applied, this theory of development can streamline cost structures, increase wages, improve trade competitiveness and protect the environment. The Vietnam Chamber of Commerce and Industry, Ministry of Natural Resources and Environment, Ministry of Foreign Affairs, and Ministry of Science and Technology are all on board with this philosophy.[12] At the same time, Vietnam's shift from a centrally planned economy to a market economy makes renewable development possible.

While US government backing is essential, the engine room of this effort should be free enterprise, which means creative corporate America. The US Business Council for Sustainable Development, an arm of the World Business Council for Sustainable Development, might make a good organising mechanism. While the United States and Vietnam would assume the lead roles, the design and pursuit of renewable development should square with evolving approaches of international financial institutions. The World Bank in particular could offer highly relevant lessons gleaned from extensive experience for fostering Vietnamese economic reform, and has provided substantial financing for its development over three decades. The private–public strategy advocated here would benefit crucially from ongoing World Bank expertise and commitment.

*   *   *

Even without entering a US-led defence alliance, Vietnam's new-found economic prowess and partnerships with the United States, Japan and others could prompt an angry and disruptive Chinese reaction. Given the dismal results of its wolf-warrior diplomacy, however, Beijing can ill afford to alienate any of its neighbours. While China is more likely to court than contest Vietnam's rise, its state-heavy system is no longer a model for Vietnam or other countries in the region. Beijing's growing enmity towards independent private enterprise cuts against the track Vietnam should and apparently prefers to take.

The United States, however, would be unlikely to take an active role in helping Vietnam improve productivity and exploit its exceptional resources and location if domestic US audiences saw such an agenda as yet another foreign burden on US resources, especially given the demands and dangers in Europe and the Middle East. American policymakers must therefore cast US-centred development assistance to Vietnam as part of a robust approach, fusing public and private efforts, to quelling China's destabilising activities in East Asia.

The framework and guiding principles announced by American and Vietnamese leaders last September suggest the right mindset and sense of balance. US President Joe Biden and General Secretary of the Communist Party of Vietnam Central Committee Nguyen Phu Trong pledged to elevate their nations' implementation of a 'Comprehensive Strategic Partnership' to advance peace and development. They are calling for collaboration on diplomacy, trade and investment, science and technological innovation, education, the environment, health and cultural exchanges. With respect to defence, the emphasis is, as it should be, on maritime security, transnational crime, human and drug trafficking, counter-terrorism and cyber crime.[13] As a matter of diplomatic prudence, the leaders have not mentioned an alliance against China. But a joint call for renewable development involving US and Vietnamese enterprises would further strengthen bilateral ties and, without unduly antagonising China, draw Vietnam closer to the Quad's orbit.

Notes

[1] For an alternative to such a vulnerable concentration of forces, see David C. Gompert and Martin Libicki, 'Detect and Engage: A New American Way of War', *Survival*, vol. 65, no. 5, October–November 2023, pp. 65–74.

[2] Richard Wike et al., 'The Tarnished American Brand', Pew Research Center, 26 June 2017, https://www.pewresearch.org/global/2017/06/26/tarnished-american-brand/.

[3] See Sharon Seah and Indira Zahra Aridati, 'Vietnamese Perceptions in a Changing Sino-US Relationship', *Fulcrum: Analysis on Southeast Asia*, 15 September 2023, https://fulcrum.sg/vietnamese-perceptions-in-a-changing-sino-us-relationship/.

[4] See Center for Strategic and International Studies, 'How Much Trade Transits the South China Sea?', ChinaPower, https://chinapower.csis.org/much-trade-transits-south-china-sea/.

[5] According to a 2023 Gallup International survey of people in 54 countries, the Vietnamese, at 86%, were in fact the most optimistic. Gallup

International, 'Not Much of a Free World. But At Least Optimistic', 16 May 2023, https://www.gallup-international.com/survey-results-and-news/survey-result/not-much-of-a-free-world-but-at-least-optimistic.

6   Office of the US Trade Representative, 'Vietnam', https://ustr.gov/countries-regions/southeast-asia-pacific/vietnam.

7   See, for example, Darrelle Ng, 'China's Slower Growth Expected as Economy Matures; Increase in Defence Spending Likely to Continue: Analysts', Channel News Asia, 6 March 2023, https://cna.asia/3Zu1ZPF.

8   See Embassy of India in Hanoi, Vietnam, 'Trade and Economic Relations', https://www.indembassyhanoi.gov.in/page/economic-and-commercial/; Australian Government, Department of Foreign Affairs and Trade, 'Vietnam Country Brief', https://www.dfat.gov.au/geo/vietnam/vietnam-country-brief; and 'Vietnam's Trade with Largest Partners in 2022', Vietnam+, 14 February 2023, https://en.vietnamplus.vn/vietnams-trade-with-biggest-partners-in-2022/248239.vnp.

9   Observatory of Economic Complexity, 'China', https://oec.world/en/profile/country/chn.

10 See United Nations, 'United Nations Conference on Environment and Development, Rio de Janeiro, Brazil, 3–14 June 1992', https://www.un.org/en/conferences/environment/rio1992.

11 Also known as 'sustainable development' – a term that we think does not fully capture the new approach needed.

12 See 'Việt Nam to Host Green Growth, Global Goals Partnership Summit in 2025', *Việt Nam News*, 26 September 2023, https://vietnamnews.vn/environment/1594298/viet-nam-to-host-green-growth-global-goals-partnership-summit-in-2025.html.

13 See White House, 'Joint Leaders' Statement: Elevating United States–Vietnam Relations to a Comprehensive Strategic Partnership', 11 September 2023, https://www.whitehouse.gov/briefing-room/statements-releases/2023/09/11/joint-leaders-statement-elevating-united-states-vietnam-relations-to-a-comprehensive-strategic-partnership/.

Noteworthy

The Manama Dialogue and the Gaza war

'Let me be extremely clear what matters to the Kingdom of Bahrain. There must be no forced displacement of Palestinians in Gaza, now or ever. There must be no reoccupation. There must be no reduction in Gaza's territory. And on the other side, there must be no terrorism directed from Gaza against the Israeli public … Central to finding that two-state solution is that the Palestinian people's hopes and aspirations must be at the centre of any post-crisis government.

In the immediate aftermath of the war, conditions must be set to deliver elections … Elections will lead … to a strong, unified leadership across Gaza and the West Bank that can deliver hope and prosperity to the Palestinian people for years to come. And not only that, this organisation – this process, must lead to a serious interlocutor and partner in delivering a just and lasting peace with a viable and independent Palestinian state as its goal, and also deliver security and stability to its Israeli neighbour.'

Prince Salman bin Hamad bin Isa Al Khalifa, Crown Prince of the Kingdom of Bahrain, delivers the keynote address at the 19th IISS Manama Dialogue on 17 November 2023.[1]

'The conflict … did not start on 7 October … For years we have been warning against the absence of a political horizon. For years we have been warning that the blockage of any horizon towards solving the Palestinian–Israeli conflict is going to drag us exactly into this moment. For years we have been saying the fallacy of assuming that you can parachute over the Palestinian issue to create regional peace is wrong, it will only bring disaster, and here we are. Show me who is talking about any regional project at this point, who is talking about integration.

[…]

What will Gaza produce after this? Israel says, again, it wants to wipe out Hamas … Hamas is an idea. You cannot bomb an idea out of existence. If you are not happy with [what] Hamas is doing, convince the Palestinian people that they have a future and that Hamas is standing between them and that future. Thus far … reality has not shown that. Palestinian people have been left with nothing left to lose on the West Bank and in Gaza. Are we not going to learn?'

Ayman Safadi, Jordan's deputy prime minister and minister of foreign affairs and expatriates, speaks at the 19th IISS Manama Dialogue on 18 November.[2]

'We have to keep in mind – and we do – that Hamas started this war.

[…]

In the near term, the US insists and will work to ensure the following with respect to Gaza. Firstly, there must be no forcible displacement of Palestinians from Gaza. Secondly, there must be no reoccupation of Gaza. Thirdly, there must be no reduction of the territory of Gaza. This is Palestinian land, and it must remain Palestinian land. Fourthly, Gaza must not be used as a platform for terrorism or other violent acts. That means no threats to Israel from Gaza. Finally, there must be no besiegement of Gaza. The innocent people of Gaza must be separated from Hamas. They are not responsible for its crimes.

Survival | vol. 66 no. 1 | February–March 2024 | pp. 66–68   https://doi.org/10.1080/00396338.2024.2309075

[…]

Our five no's … are followed by five affirmative and forward-looking principles: Firstly, the Palestinian people and their voices and aspirations must be at the centre of post-crisis governance in Gaza. Secondly, the West Bank and Gaza must return to unified governance, ultimately under a revitalised Palestinian Authority, and be incorporated into a future Palestinian state … Thirdly, Israel must be secure … Fourthly, resources must be provided, and we must prepare now to support the post-crisis phase in Gaza to include interim security resources as necessary within the paradigm that we have laid out … Fifth, a reconstruction mechanism must be established to ensure the needs of Gazans are met on a long-term and sustainable basis.'
Brett McGurk, coordinator for the Middle East and North Africa for the US National Security Council, speaks at the 19th IISS Manama Dialogue on 18 November.[3]

Red Sea turbulence

'In response to continued illegal, dangerous, and destabilizing Houthi attacks against vessels, including commercial shipping, transiting the Red Sea, the armed forces of the United States and United Kingdom, with support from the Netherlands, Canada, Bahrain, and Australia, conducted joint strikes in accordance with the inherent right of individual and collective self-defense, consistent with the UN Charter, against a number of targets in Houthi-controlled areas of Yemen. These precision strikes were intended to disrupt and degrade the capabilities the Houthis use to threaten global trade and the lives of international mariners in one of the world's most critical waterways.

The Houthis' more than two dozen attacks on commercial vessels since mid-November constitute an international challenge. Today's action demonstrated a shared commitment to freedom of navigation, international commerce, and defending the lives of mariners from illegal and unjustifiable attacks.

Our aim remains to de-escalate tensions and restore stability in the Red Sea, but let our message be clear: we will not hesitate to defend lives and protect the free flow of commerce in one of the world's most critical waterways in the face of continued threats.'
The governments of Australia, Bahrain, Canada, Denmark, Germany, the Netherlands, New Zealand, South Korea, the United Kingdom and the United States issue a joint statement on 11 January 2024.[4]

'President [Joe] Biden's decision to use military force against these Iranian proxies is overdue. I am hopeful these operations mark an enduring shift in the Biden administration's approach to Iran and its proxies.'
United States Senate Republican leader Mitch McConnell comments on the strikes in Yemen on 11 January.[5]

'The President needs to come to Congress before launching a strike against the Houthis in Yemen and involving us in another middle east conflict. That is Article I of the Constitution. I will stand up for that regardless of whether a Democrat or Republican is in the White House.'
US Representative Ro Khanna posts to X on 11 January.[6]

'The American and British enemies bear full responsibility for their criminal aggression against our Yemeni people. It will not go unpunished or unanswered. The Yemeni armed forces will not hesitate to target threatening sources and all hostile targets on land and sea, in order to defend Yemen, its sovereignty and independence.'
Yahya Sarea, a spokesperson for the Houthi military, releases a statement on 12 January.[7]

'All that has been done is a disproportionate use of force. At the moment, they [the US and UK] are trying to turn the Red Sea into a sea of blood.'

Turkish President Recep Tayyip Erdoğan.[8]

Kissinger's thoughts

'The relationship of America to China is an essential element of such an approach and of international order. The prospects of global peace and order may well depend on it. Many writers have drawn an analogy between China's emergence as a great power and potential rival of the United States today and Germany's ascendancy in Europe a hundred years ago, when Great Britain was the dominant international power but proved unable to integrate Germany.

The case of China is even more complicated. It is not an issue of integrating a European-style nation-state but a full-fledged continental power. China's ascendancy is accompanied by massive socio-economic change and, in some instances, dislocation internally. China's ability to continue to manage its emergence as a great power side by side with its internal transformation is one of the pivotal questions of our time.

Increased popular participation is not the inevitable road to international reconciliation, as is often asserted. A century ago, Germany was gradually allowing more and more freedom of speech and press. But that newfound freedom in the public sphere gave vent to an assortment of voices, including a chauvinistic tendency insisting on an ever more assertive foreign policy. Western leaders would do well to keep this in mind when hectoring China on its internal politics.

This is not the occasion to review the range of American and Chinese interactions. I would like to conclude with one general point: both countries are less nations in the European sense than continental expressions of a cultural identity. Neither has much practice in cooperative relations with equals. Yet their leaders have no more important task than to implement the truths that neither country will ever be able to dominate the other, and that conflict between them would exhaust their societies and undermine the prospects of world peace. Such a conviction is an ultimate form of realism.'

Former US secretary of state Henry Kissinger, who died on 29 November 2023, writes in the December 2010–January 2011 issue of Survival.[9]

Sources

1 Prince Salman bin Hamad bin Isa Al Khalifa, 'Keynote Address', IISS Manama Dialogue, Bahrain, 17 November 2023, https://www.iiss.org/globalassets/media-library---content--migration/files/manama-dialogue-delta/2023/final/keynote/hrh-prince-salman-bin-hamad-bin-isa-al-khalifa_keynote-address.pdf.

2 Ayman Safadi, 'First Plenary Session: War, Diplomacy and De-escalation', IISS Manama Dialogue, Bahrain, 18 November 2023, https://www.iiss.org/globalassets/media-library--content--migration/files/manama-dialogue-delta/2023/final/p1/ayman-safadi-deputy-prime-minister-and-minister-of-foreign-affairs-and-expatriates-jordan_as-delivered.pdf.

3 Brett McGurk, 'First Plenary Session: War, Diplomacy and De-escalation', IISS Manama Dialogue, 18 November 2023, https://www.iiss.org/globalassets/media-library---content--migration/files/manama-dialogue-delta/2023/final/p1/brett-mcgurk---coordinator--for-the-middle-east-and-north-africa-national-security-council-us_as-delivered.pdf.

4 White House, 'Joint Statement from the Governments of Australia, Bahrain, Canada, Denmark, Germany, Netherlands, New Zealand, Republic of Korea, United Kingdom, and the United States', 11 January 2024, https://www.whitehouse.gov/briefing-room/statements-releases/2024/01/11/joint-statement-from-the-governments-of-australia-bahrain-canada-denmark-germany-netherlands-new-zealand-republic-of-korea-united-kingdom-and-the-united-states/.

5 'World Reacts to US, UK Attacks on Houthi Targets in Yemen', Al-Jazeera, 12 January 2024, https://www.aljazeera.com/news/2024/1/12/world-reacts-to-us-uk-attacks-on-houthi-targets-in-yemen.

6 Ro Khanna (@RoKhanna), post to X, 11 January 2024, https://twitter.com/RoKhanna/status/1745590169493745693?s=20.

7 'Houthis Vow Retaliation for US and UK Airstrikes – Video', Guardian, 12 January 2024, https://www.theguardian.com/world/video/2024/jan/12/houthis-vow-retaliation-for-us-and-uk-airstrikes-video.

8 'Erdogan Accuses U.S., Britain of Trying to Turn Red Sea into "Sea of Blood"', Reuters, 12 January 2024, https://www.reuters.com/world/middle-east/erdogan-accuses-us-britain-trying-turn-red-sea-into-sea-blood-2024-01-12/.

9 Henry A. Kissinger, 'Power Shifts', Survival, vol. 52, no. 6, December 2010–January 2011, pp. 205–12.

The Battle for the Internet

Edoardo Campanella and John Haigh

For the last two centuries, great powers – both nations and associated firms – have fiercely competed to set the technical standards for leading technologies. By imposing their preferred standards, nations not only solve technical problems to their advantage, but also project power globally. Standards determine what kind of technology will become predominant, ensuring market shares and market power to the countries and companies that set them, while forcing foreign competitors to adapt at hefty cost.[1] As the industrialist Werner von Siemens reportedly put it: 'He who owns the standards, owns the market.'[2] Standards can also pay strategic dividends. The radio network that Britain established in the late nineteenth century afforded it a monopoly over radio transmissions that it used successfully in the Second World War against Germany.[3] Once a standard becomes locked in, it is rarely overturned. Today, there is no rail line that connects East Asia with Europe without at least two divergences in gauges.[4] This is because, in the nineteenth century, the Russian tsars deliberately chose a different gauge to prevent European wagons and locomotives from using Russian tracks for invasion.

The internet is heavily dependent on shared standards across multiple platforms that have evolved over decades to assure compatibility in both hardware and software. These shared standards enable highly decentralised

Edoardo Campanella is a Research Fellow at the Harvard Kennedy School's Mossavar-Rahmani Center for Business and Government and co-author of *Anglo Nostalgia: The Politics of Emotion in a Fractured West* (Oxford University Press, 2019). **John Haigh** is Co-Director of the Mossavar-Rahmani Center for Business and Government and Lecturer in Public Policy at the Harvard Kennedy School. The authors are grateful to seminar participants at the Harvard Kennedy School and other colleagues for helpful comments on previous drafts.

Survival | vol. 66 no. 1 | February–March 2024 | pp. 69–84   https://doi.org/10.1080/00396338.2024.2309076

components developed by disparate parties to integrate into a highly functional overall system. One of the inventors of the internet protocols, Vinton G. Cerf, has noted that

> from a technical standpoint, the original shared vision guiding the internet's development was that every device on the internet should be able to exchange data packets with any other device that was willing to receive them. Universal connectivity among the willing was the default assumption.[5]

This notion was based on a commitment to a unified cyberspace that would make for inter-operability across networks and a seamlessly interconnected, borderless and transparent internet.

This unified cyberspace essentially became a reality, with significant economic and geopolitical ramifications. It reduced and potentially eliminated sovereign limits on the flow of information and the power of governments to shape and control information. But countries, of course, are not unified. Nations are geographically bounded and exercise sovereignty over their territory through their legal and political institutions. The concept of a globally unified cyberspace and that of geographically bounded sovereign states are therefore misaligned.[6] Today, many states, particularly authoritarian regimes, want the state to be the basic governing structure of the internet.

China, in particular, is now proposing a fundamentally new internet protocol — the so-called 'New IP'. It is intended to build 'intrinsic security' into the web, but will also generate the capacity for China to wield a massive surveillance system. Intrinsic security means that individuals must register to go online, and that authorities can both observe the online activities of individuals and shut off an individual user's internet access at any time.[7] In their 2021 'Digital and Technology Ministerial Declaration', however, G7 member countries created the Framework for G7 Collaboration on Digital Technical Standards, which referred to internet protocols and technical standards for emerging technologies as areas that 'could affect … our shared values as open and democratic societies'.[8] This tension is an entirely new chapter in the history of technical standard-setting that will help shape the relationship between China and the West.

The West has so far resisted any movement towards the Chinese model. But China is unlikely to back down, because the debate involves not merely technical disagreements, but also differing visions of the world – decentralised and democratic versus centralised and authoritarian.

The traditional internet

Since the dawn of the First Industrial Revolution, setting standards has traditionally been a prerogative of technical experts, largely from the private sector.[9] In the nineteenth century, they began to establish standard-setting committees within national professional and industry associations. Then, in the early twentieth century and especially after the Second World War, standardisation became an international matter. For instance, the standardisation of shipping containers in the 1970s contributed mightily to advanced globe-spanning commerce. However, for the most critical technologies – particularly those related to the defence sector, such as radio frequencies or track gauges – national governments increasingly intervened in private negotiations, with political considerations often trumping technical ones.

The internet has developed differently. From 1969 to 2000, its evolution did not follow the historical pattern from national to international. The dominant vision and ideology of the internet community resisted conventional government regulation.[10] By virtue of its open and international nature, the internet was often portrayed as or presumed to be insusceptible to regulation. That said, despite widespread rhetorical support for a sort of 'cyber anarchy', the internet has always been subject to a set of open standards and platforms with many deeply engaged stakeholders – firms, governments, academics and non-profits.[11] They have steadily improved upon its basic architecture by adding new functionalities in the public domain.

The internet is truly a network of networks. Its main components are private networks, defined as autonomous systems with the capacity to determine who can access what information, but with the ability to share information through common standards. The internet has evolved on the basis of a modular structure requiring collaboration and coordination among multiple parties. The modules are part of a protocol stack – a term used by engineers to describe the many layers in a packet-switched network. Each layer handles a different set of tasks associated with networked communications (for example, address assignment, session managing and congestion control). Engineers focusing on a particular layer need only be concerned with implementation details at that layer, because the functions or services provided by other layers are prescribed by their own standards.

Accordingly, a line is implicitly drawn between application layers, where humans and technologies interface, and the core architectural layers, where data is transmitted. The application layers are inherently political. Think about someone chatting on Facebook or watching a YouTube video. Communications take place at that level and, if the layer is centrally controlled, governments could limit freedom of expression and thought, impinging on the privacy of an individual and targeting specific groups.

The model of open and modular standards has been characterised by pluralistic, voluntary, bottom-up participation, driven by innovation.[12] Key organisations, composed mostly of engineers, have coalesced to develop shared standards.[13] Three standards-development organisations (SDOs) are key: the Internet Engineering Task Force (IETF), which shaped the infrastructure layer; the Institute of Electrical and Electronics Engineers (IEEE), which shaped local network and wireless communications; and the World Wide Web Consortium (W3C), which shaped the web-based software and application layer. One of their most noteworthy collective achievements is the iconic Internet Protocol Suite (TCP/IP), first developed by Bob Kahn and Cerf as part of a US Advanced Research Projects Agency Network initiative in the early 1970s and progressively refined.

The TCP/IP was introduced to allow physically distinct networks to interconnect with one another as 'peers' in order to exchange packets through special hardware.[14] In this structure, operators of different components of the system cannot observe all the aspects of the information sent. An email, for example, is broken into packets, and the entities moving the packets through the system are unable to access their content. The identities of the sending and receiving parties are also encrypted and protected through the Domain Name System (DNS). Messages that move from one computer to another are broken down into small packets, each of which is stamped with the IP address of the computer it wants to reach. Eventually, the receiving computer reassembles the packets in the correct order. Thus, the current system is akin to a postman who delivers envelopes along his route without knowing what's inside them. Only the final recipient of the mail can piece the packets back together and read the message in its entirety.

A new battleground

The current highly decentralised internet system is compatible with the democratic leanings of Western countries. Even so, many democratic countries are interested in making the system more amenable to regulation to reduce the influence of Big Tech, while giving intelligence agencies greater access to users' personal data.[15] It is rumoured that the United States government has pressured multi-stakeholder organisations into introducing a new IP protocol with less extensive encryption technology.[16]

China is going a step further, however. Since 2014, President Xi Jinping has framed becoming a 'cyber great power' as the cornerstone of China's internet policy.[17] His goal is to create a 'community of common destiny in cyberspace', based on a redesigned global internet infrastructure and overhauled internet-governance norms. If China can set the standards, it can better manage its technology and networks, thus supporting national security. China's aspiration is to embed its own ideological tenets into the design and architecture of new technologies, with economic benefits flowing to the most capable and successful Chinese firms.[18]

This effort is part of Beijing's broader campaign to evolve from standard-taker to standard-maker in key industrial domains, from emerging high-tech fields such as 5G, artificial intelligence, the Internet of Things and smart cities to traditional sectors including energy, healthcare, railways and agriculture. A popular Chinese adage is that 'third-tier companies make products, second-tier companies make technology, first-tier companies make standards'.[19] Beijing is trying to shift the development of the internet standards from the multi-stakeholder, collaborative, voluntary consensus system implemented by the IETF, IEEE, W3C and related organisations to a multilateral, state-driven forum like the United Nations' International Telecommunication Union (ITU).[20] Unlike the open-standard model, the ITU restricts negotiations to member states. In 2021, Russia and China issued a joint statement asserting that 'all States have equal rights to participate in global-network governance, increasing their role in this process and preserving the sovereign right of States to regulate the national segment of the internet', and calling for an enhanced role for the ITU and increased representation of China and Russia in its governing bodies.[21] Beijing exerted strenuous efforts to elevate a Russian candidate and a former Huawei executive to the position of ITU secretary-general in autumn 2022, though Doreen Bogdan-Martin, the American candidate, was overwhelmingly elected, receiving 139 out of 172 votes cast.[22]

While the ITU formally operates on the UN's one-nation-one-vote basis, member states assign representatives to develop and recommend standards in ITU forums. In recent years, Chinese nationals have participated in very large numbers. US private-industry representatives have been fewer and fewer, as not many US companies have been inclined to address the infrastructure of the internet.[23] China's alternative infrastructure would introduce new controls between elements of the protocol stack and network connections. This trend has left China in a position to exercise significant influence in the process.

The ITU Regulations have treaty status, which means that the countries that have signed them have a legal obligation to adhere to them. Russia customarily has tried to promote changes to the regulations that would apply them more explicitly to the internet and render it subject to multilateral, in this case ITU, control. The most recent effort to amend the regulations occurred in 2012 at the World Conference on International Telecommunications in Dubai. There, a majority of countries agreed to changes that arguably moved the internet a little closer to centralised control, but many countries, including the US, reserved the right to disregard them. As a result, the democratic countries generally are not bound by the amendments, and the effort to increase centralisation failed.[24]

Because trade agreements tend to be more open to states that adopt international standards within multilateral bodies like the ITU, intergovernmental standardisation helps secure trade protection for new technologies. According to existing World Trade Organization (WTO) rules, 'technical regulations in accordance with relevant international standards are rebuttably presumed not to create an unnecessary obstacle to international trade'.[25] Therefore, once a Chinese-devised standard were approved at the ITU, Beijing would be able to export its own internet-related technologies to third parties as part of its Digital Silk Road initiative with little further scrutiny.

China's New IP

China's primary vehicle for advocating for new internet standards has been the Chinese tech company Huawei. In September 2019, the company submitted to the ITU's Telecommunication Standardization Advisory Group a proposal for the creation of a series of technical standards underpinning a new, centralised internet architecture – the New IP. Similar technical proposals were made at SDOs such as the IETF. Both the ITU and the SDOs rejected the proposals, but China has since been working on domestic pilots for the New IP. The large-scale effort appears to have started in April 2021, with the announcement of a backbone network that will connect 40 leading Chinese universities to test what has been advertised as the 'internet of the future'.

China's plan is to improve these standards domestically and legitimise them internationally, which would yield a proof of concept, at least among the authoritarian regimes that would be the most natural adopters. In form, this is in line with the traditional model of developing standards nationally and proliferating them internationally. Iran, Russia and Saudi Arabia already support China's internet vision, and it has recently focused the World Internet Conference, which China founded and controls, on shifting authority away from Western-dominated institutions.[26] Beijing is also working on new internet standards that could be appealing to the Global South, specifically in the context of the Digital Silk Road.

The New IP is supposed to connect devices and share information and resources across networks through centralised control of the transferred data. Its champions cast the old IP as outdated. It is true that the current form of IP address was designed to identify only physical objects such as personal computers and mobile handsets bound to specific locations, whereas the evolving Internet of Things is connecting an expanding range of virtual entities, including sensors, content and services.[27] The traditional IP does not incorporate the identification of the content or services it carries, which hinders it from providing the most efficient means of transmitting information.

China's alternative internet infrastructure would introduce new controls at the level of the network connection. Individuals would operate on a blockchain infrastructure in which the network activities were tracked with an indelible record. Furthermore, a network operator would be able to identify who sent the information, its specific content and nature, and who received it, and have the ability to stop the dissemination of the information and block access to it.

The dark side of China's proposal

When the first postal system was established in the United Kingdom in 1657, the parliamentary act that created the General Post Office stated that its mission was 'to discover and prevent many dangerous and wicked designs which have been and are daily contrived against the peace and welfare of this Commonwealth'.[28] In other words, postal workers were initially allowed to read letters on behalf of the king. As civilisation evolved, privacy was increasingly recognised and enforced. In effect, China now wants to allow postal workers to open letters, see what's inside them, and then decide whether or not to deliver them to their destinations. If its proposals are adopted, the internet risks moving in a decidedly retrograde direction.

From China's standpoint, the New IP can be seen as a technical solution to a political problem. Since it would jettison privacy standards for data collection, a centralised authority would be able to track the browsing history and the online habits of any individual or entity, while deciding who could access the internet.[29] These features would make the New IP into an instrument of social control and state surveillance. In countries run by authoritarian regimes, losing anonymity on the internet would endanger the lives of human-rights activists, independent journalists and political opponents. They could be imperilled even in illiberal democracies, especially those in which ideological polarisation were extremely high or populist leaders in power. The New IP would facilitate far-reaching censorship and propaganda.

In the Chinese domestic context, surveillance does not occur through hacking, but rather is built into the internet architecture itself. Compiled digital records for businesses and individuals feed into the so-called Social Credit System, through which their trustworthiness is determined.[30] With the New IP in place, Beijing would be able to erect a vastly more sophisticated version of the increasingly porous 'Great Firewall', which was introduced more than two decades ago to stop citizens from connecting to banned foreign websites – such as Google and the *New York Times* – and to block politically sensitive domestic content and prevent mass organising online.[31]

China is likely to keep investing in its New IP and to gain the support of other authoritarian regimes. Since the West would not support any such standard, there is a growing risk of the internet's fragmentation – sometimes called 'splinternet' – with a traditional, largely decentralised architecture on one side and a centralised one that does not respect the values and norms of open societies on the other. But even among those governments that opt for the Chinese model, there would be the risk of a lack of inter-operability. When crossing national boundaries, individuals would be compelled to ask for permission to connect to the local internet provider, and administrators could have the power to deny access. Rather than a unified World Wide Web, a patchwork of national internets, each with its own rules and potentially significant restrictions on the free flow of information, would emerge. While governments do have some control over access to websites today, the control under China's New IP would be significantly greater.

This disposition would be consistent with the idea of cyber sovereignty that Beijing outlined in its 2017 International Strategy of Cooperation on Cyberspace, stating that 'countries should respect each other's right to choose their own path of cyber development, model of cyber regulation and internet public policies, and participate in international cyberspace governance on an equal footing'.[32] Cyber sovereignty is also one of the 15 guiding principles of the Digital Silk Road.

It remains likely that the SDOs – the IETF, IEEE, W3C and related organisations – will continue to exercise considerable control over internet standards. Even if China implements the New IP within China, it will still need to meet existing standards and accommodate the structure of the internet at points of interconnection if it wishes to maintain the flow of information across sovereign boundaries. It has little choice but to do this to a degree, given that a healthy international flow of data is essential to sustaining the integrated global supply chains on which China's economic strength crucially depends. But global information flows would still enable China to establish an expanded global-surveillance system, with implications for national security, financial flows and stability, and individual privacy.

To implant a truly new internet, China would have to convince a substantial number of the world's governments and populations of its advantages over the existing internet structure. At present, this appears an unlikely proposition. But to decisively preclude China's eventual success, Western democracies – through both public and private institutions – must close ranks more than they have done so far to entrench the historical multi-stakeholder approach to developing and evolving internet standards.

A new approach

The core issue is whether the United States, other democratic countries and associated private companies have the will and capacity to build a 'coalition of the willing' to develop standards in key technology areas that support democratic values, as well as a robust competitive market. From a technical standpoint, the traditional IP system based on TCP/IP requires substantial upgrades. At the host level, it suffers from insufficient memory and inadequate information processors, causing slow speeds and delays in the transfer of data across networks (so-called latency problems). At the IP layer of the protocol stack, there are problems with discarding data packets in transmission and in reassembling them at the receiver end. This occurs, for example, when a received packet has a transmission or format error, or when the receiving device does not have enough storage room for it. Internet users then cannot access the content they want.

Even so, over the last 40 years, the layered and modular architecture of the internet has proved extremely adaptable, incorporating new networking technologies, meeting new requirements and supporting an exponentially growing number of users. The modular character of the internet architecture allows for innovation in one area without having to redesign the entire internet.[33] Lower layers (such as physical media) can evolve without the necessity of modifying the upper-layer applications, and vice versa. The introduction of new wireless technologies does not require a universal upgrade.

Western powers, and the US government in particular, could exploit the technical flexibility of the TCP/IP to propose internet upgrades within the existing framework, drawing in the private sector to build a common front for ameliorating technical shortcomings. The critical entities for carrying forward such an effort are the existing SDOs that have developed internet standards, whose processes are generally robust. The process should remain consensus-driven, and the standards voluntary and non-binding, to provide a hedge against the actions of countries pushing standards that are inconsistent with democratic values and detrimental to companies operating in global markets. The challenge will be to find common ground between the European Union and the US, as their underlying philosophies for internet governance are not always fully aligned – especially when it comes to regulating certain areas of the internet, less so when it comes to its architecture.

In addition, democracies should incentivise key parties to participate more extensively in the SDO standard-setting processes – especially in the technical committees and working groups. These parties include company engineers, researchers, academics and, in some cases, public officials. In this vein, it is worth noting that the Chinese government provides subsidies and technical consultation to Chinese firms to strengthen proposals they submit to international SDOs.[34]

In April 2022, the 'Declaration for the Future of the Internet', spearheaded by the EU and the United States, was promulgated. Signed by more than 60 countries, the document affirmed the objective of preserving an 'open, free, global, interoperable, reliable, and secure' internet.[35] Most, however, were democracies. Thus, the inability of the West to promote a vision for the internet that is appealing to emerging economies and unstable democracies – and the risk of splinternet – remain. India, which is formally a democracy despite clear authoritarian regression, has not signed the document and is introducing its own localised controls, though it has resisted Chinese digital initiatives.[36] Winning the substantial support of New Delhi is key to putting Western-designed internet governance on the right track.

* * *

It is in the West's interest to engage China in dialogue to avoid the internet's costly fragmentation. Western democratic governments should work concertedly to nurture an internet that is consistent with democratic values and Western social norms. But it seems unavoidable that Western governments too will increasingly want to protect the data of their citizens, build walls against cyber attacks, minimise fake news and tame the power of tech companies as a matter of national sovereignty. Accordingly, the logical way forward is to strike a balance between the old multi-stakeholder approach and the intergovernmental one that is promoted by Beijing.

One approach would be to have a layered governance system, with the first layer featuring technical discussions among experts within the traditional internet-related bodies and the second bringing together governments to address selected issues related to national sovereignty and security. It might be possible to find common ground on general principles with authoritarian regimes. The United Nations has an important role to play through its Envoy on Technology and the UN-based Internet Governance Forum, as well as the ITU. They should monitor the ongoing geopolitical contest over internet governance and flag possible privacy, civil- and political-rights violations arising from technological standards under consideration by multilateral bodies. In this vein, with the encouragement of Western democracies, the WTO could more aggressively influence the evolution of the internet through its e-commerce working group.

The WTO Agreement on Technical Barriers to Trade is intended to prevent member countries from using domestic technical standards to protect local firms by requiring member countries to use international standards rather than domestic ones.[37] But that only works when the SDOs operate by broad consensus, such that it is not necessary to renegotiate technical standards in the context of trade negotiations. Through organisations such as the ITU, China is attempting to bootstrap its own domestic standards into international ones, with an eye to requiring foreign companies operating in China to use new ITU international standards to their detriment. Incorporating firmer consensual constraints on such standards – including those regarding individual rights – would diminish China's incentives for manipulating the standard-setting process and improve prospects for acceptable mutual accommodation. Over the last couple of centuries, there have been many examples of technical standards that have shaped great-power dynamics. Never have they been as consequential as those for the governance of the internet.

Notes

1   See, for example, John Seaman, 'China and the New Geopolitics of Technical Standardization', *Notes de l'Ifri*, January 2020, https://www.ifri.org/sites/default/files/atoms/files/seaman_china_standardization_2020.pdf.

2   Quoted in Hermann J. Koch, *Practical Guide to International Standardization for Electrical Engineers: Impact on Smart Grid and E-mobility Markets* (Hoboken, NJ: Wiley, 2016), p. xix.

3   See Markus Brunnermeier, Rush Doshi and Harold James, 'Beijing's Bismarckian Ghost: How Great Powers Compete Economically', *Washington Quarterly*, vol. 41, no. 3, Fall 2018, pp. 161–6.

4   See Richard Mowbray Haywood, *The Beginnings of Railway Development in Russia in the Reign of Nicholas I, 1835–1842* (Durham, NC: Duke University Press, 1969).

5   See William J. Drake, Vinton G. Cerf and Wolfgang Kleinwächter, 'Internet Fragmentation: An Overview', Future of the Internet Initiative White Paper, World Economic Forum, January 2016, p. 2, https://www3.weforum.org/docs/WEF_FII_Internet_Fragmentation_An_Overview_2016.pdf.

6   See Milton Mueller, *Will the Internet Fragment?* (London: Polity Press, 2017).

7   See Mark Montgomery and Theo Lebryk, 'China's Dystopian "New IP" Plan Shows Need for Renewed US Commitment to Internet Governance', *Just Security*, 13 April 2021, https://www.justsecurity.org/75741/chinas-dystopian-new-ip-plan-shows-need-for-renewed-us-commitment-to-internet-governance/.

8   G7, 'Framework for G7 Collaboration on Digital and Technical Standards', G7 Digital and Technology Track – Annex 1, 2021, http://www.g8.utoronto.ca/ict/2021-Annex_1_Framework_for_G7_collaboration_on_Digital_Technical_Standards.pdf.

9   See JoAnne Yates and Craig Murphy, *Engineering Rules: Global Standard Setting Since 1880* (Baltimore, MD: Johns Hopkins University Press, 2019).

10   See Philip J. Weiser, 'Internet Governance, Standard Setting, and Self-regulation', *Northern Kentucky Law Review*, vol. 28, no. 4, 2001, pp. 822–46.

11   See Jack L. Goldsmith, 'Against Cyberanarchy', *University of Chicago Law Review*, vol. 65, no. 4, Autumn 1998, pp. 1,199–250.

12   See Konstantinos Karachalios and Karen McCabe, 'Standards, Innovation and Their Role in the Context of the World Trade Organization', International Centre for Trade and Sustainable Development and World Economic Forum, December 2013, https://issuu.com/ictsd/docs/e15_trade_and_innovation_-_karachal.

13   See Internet Society, 'Internet Governance: Why the

Multistakeholder Approach
Works', April 2016, https://
www.internetsociety.org/
wp-content/uploads/2016/04/
IG-MultiStakeholderApproach.pdf.

14 See David C. Mowery and
Timothy Simcoe, 'Is the Internet a
US Invention? An Economic and
Technological History of Computer
Networking', *Research Policy*, vol. 31,
nos 8–9, December 2002, pp. 1,369–87.

15 See Madhumita Murgia and Anna
Gross, 'Inside China's Controversial
Mission to Reinvent the Internet',
Financial Times, 27 March 2020,
https://www.ft.com/content/
ba94c2bc-6e27-11ea-9bca-bf503995cd6f.

16 Author conversation with Bruce
Schneier, Fellow at the Berkman-
Klein Center for Internet and Society,
Harvard University, and Adjunct
Lecturer at Harvard Kennedy School,
October 2023.

17 See Rush Doshi at al., 'China as a
"Cyber Great Power": Beijing's Two
Voices in Telecommunications',
Brookings Institution, April 2021,
https://www.brookings.edu/research/
china-as-a-cyber-great-power-beijings-
two-voices-in-telecommunications/.

18 See Tai Ming Cheung, 'The Rise of
China as a Cybersecurity Industrial
Power: Balancing National Security,
Geopolitical, and Development
Priorities', *Journal of Cyber Policy*, vol.
3, no. 3, December 2018, pp. 306–26.

19 Quoted in Dan Breznitz and Michael
Murphree, 'Technology Standards
in China', ETLA Brief 3, Research
Institute of the Finnish Economy, 7
February 2013.

20 See Kristen Cordell, 'The International
Telecommunication Union: The

Most Important UN Agency You
Have Never Heard Of', Center
for Strategic and International
Studies, 14 December 2020,
https://www.csis.org/analysis/
international-telecommunication-
union-most-important-un-agency-
you-have-never-heard.

21 See Simon Sharwood, 'UN's ITU
Election May Spell the End of Our
Open Internet', *Register*, 29 September
2022, https://www.theregister.
com/2022/09/29/itu_plenipotentiary_
open_internet_fight/.

22 ITU, 'Member States Elect Doreen
Bogdan-Martin as ITU Secretary-
General', 29 September 2022, https://
www.itu.int/en/mediacentre/Pages/
PR-2022-09-29-ITU-SG-elected-
Doreen-Bogdan-Martin.aspx.

23 Author conversation with Philip
Verveer, former US ambassador to
the ITU.

24 *Ibid.*

25 World Trade Organization, 'Technical
Information on Technical Barriers to
Trade', https://www.wto.org/english/
tratop_e/tbt_e/tbt_info_e.htm.

26 Konstantinos Komaitis, 'Protecting
the Open Internet from China's
Latest Governance Body', Brookings
Institution, 4 August 2022, https://
www.brookings.edu/articles/
protecting-the-open-internet-from-
chinas-latest-governance-body/.

27 See, for example, Zhe Chen et al.,
'NEW IP Framework and Protocol for
Future Applications', 2020 IEEE/IFIP
Network Operations and Management
Symposium, 2020, pp. 1–5.

28 Great Britain Philatelic Society,
'Postage of England, Scotland, and
Ireland setled [*sic*] (1657 c.30, 9th June

1657)', https://www.gbps.org.uk/information/sources/acts/1657-06-09_Act-1657-Commonwealth-cap-30.php.

29 See Stacie Hoffmann, Dominique Lazanski and Emily Taylor, 'Standardising the Splinternet: How China's Technical Standards Could Fragment the Internet', *Journal of Cyber Policy*, vol. 5, no. 2, August 2020, pp. 239–64.

30 Alexandra Stevenson and Paul Mozur, 'China Scores Businesses, and Low Grades Could Be a Trade-war Weapon', *New York Times*, 22 September 2019 (updated 23 September 2019), https://www.nytimes.com/2019/09/22/business/china-social-credit-business.html.

31 See James Griffiths, *The Great Firewall of China: How to Build and Control an Alternative Version of the Internet* (London: Zed Books, 2021). The Great Firewall is not necessarily effective if parties have access to, for example, virtual private networks.

32 For more details on China's digital sovereignty, see Xinchuchu Gao, 'Sovereignty and Cyberspace: China's Ambition to Shape Cyber Norms', LSE Blog, 18 August 2022, https://blogs.lse.ac.uk/cff/2022/08/18/sovereignty-and-cyberspace-chinas-ambition-to-shape-cyber-norms/.

33 See Internet Society, 'Huawei's "New IP" Proposal – Frequently Asked Questions', 22 February 2022, https://www.internetsociety.org/resources/doc/2022/huaweis-new-ip-proposal-faq/.

34 See Matt Sheehan and Jacob Feldgoise, 'What Washington Gets Wrong About China and Technical Standards', Carnegie Endowment for International Peace, 27 February 2023, https://carnegieendowment.org/2023/02/27/what-washington-gets-wrong-about-china-and-technical-standards-pub-89110.

35 US Department of State, 'Declaration for the Future of the Internet', https://www.state.gov/declaration-for-the-future-of-the-internet.

36 See 'India Stays Out of Global Declaration on Future on Internet', *Hindu*, 29 April 2022, https://www.thehindubusinessline.com/info-tech/white-house-60-global-partners-launch-the-declaration-of-the-future-of-the-internet-india-not-on-the-list/article65366407.ece.

37 See World Trade Organization, 'Agreement on Technical Barriers to Trade', https://www.wto.org/english/docs_e/legal_e/17-tbt.pdf.

How to Think About Risks in US Military Innovation

Kendrick Kuo

New technologies such as artificial intelligence, autonomous systems, robotics, advanced manufacturing, quantum science and hypersonic weapons are threatening to cripple existing military capabilities or render them obsolete. An ominous sense has arisen in the US military that American forces as presently constituted are inadequate to meet future security challenges and in danger of falling farther behind. Military innovation is therefore seen as a key to future victory.[1] The thinking runs that only by implementing dramatic changes in the conduct of warfare – technological, organisational, doctrinal or ideally a combination of all three – will the United States be able to maintain its military edge against great-power rivals and secure its position atop the global hierarchy. While innovation is often equated with progress, however, military innovation does not guarantee improved performance.

Military innovation is a balancing act between destroying traditional ways of war and creating new ones. It is also a gamble that risks destroying more than it creates. The more creative the destruction, the greater the risk.[2] The US armed services are betting on new capabilities and associated concepts of operation to significantly improve their combat efficiency – to meet the United States' global commitments with relatively constrained resources. But in doing so, they are also taking the risk that new ways of war

Kendrick Kuo is an assistant professor in the Strategic and Operational Research Department at the US Naval War College. The views expressed in this article are those of the author and do not necessarily represent those of the US Department of Defense or its components.

Survival | vol. 66 no. 1 | February–March 2024 | pp. 85–98   https://doi.org/10.1080/00396338.2024.2309077

might not pan out or compensate adequately for the loss of current ones. When the US Air Force bet on air-to-air missiles, it got rid of guns on fighters, only to discover that guns are useful when missiles don't always work.[3]

Dynamics inherent in the innovation process make it challenging for militaries to properly manage risks. For one, military innovation is more likely to occur when these resources are scarce. Major innovation proposals also usually need to overpromise to secure the necessary support, thus setting the stage for future disappointment. These discomfiting factors are not completely escapable, but they can be better navigated.

Dangers of creative destruction

The economist Joseph Schumpeter, who introduced the concept of creative destruction, defined innovation in economic terms as a new production function that changes the rate of converting a fixed quantity of factors into products.[4] Military organisations undertake innovation intending to improve their efficiency in converting allocated resources into mission success.[5] Changes to force structure and doctrine that elevate new capabilities also downgrade older ones. The idea is that forces will thereby be better at accomplishing their assigned missions and do so at lower cost in lives, equipment or time.

Those missions are many and varied, but resources are constrained. The United States is indirectly engaged in a war with Russia in Ukraine, which continues to unfold in unpredictable ways that might trigger escalation. The People's Republic of China is investing significant resources into its own military-modernisation efforts.[6] Iran and North Korea remain potential flashpoints. At the same time, defence spending, though growing, is struggling to keep pace with inflation, let alone the growing military strength of potential enemies and the demanding requirements of projecting force across large distances into highly contested environments.

Military innovation holds out the prospect of advancing crucial missions more quickly and effectively. Thus, the US armed services are actively pursuing significant changes in force structure and doctrine. In 2019, the air force launched its *Skyborg* programme, demonstrating uncrewed combat air vehicles with an eye to providing a 'loyal wingman' capability.[7] It is also implementing its 'agile combat employment' concept to disperse aircraft and equipment across major hub bases to increase survivability by complicating enemy targeting.[8] The navy is exploring a hybrid fleet of crewed, uncrewed and optionally crewed vessels.[9] The army is restructuring its field formations to implement a new multidomain-operations doctrine.[10] Perhaps the most controversial innovation effort is the US Marine Corps' push to stand up marine littoral regiments and divest of main battle tanks, most towed cannon artillery and many air assets to modernise for distributed maritime operations.[11] Whether these moves bridge what appears to be a yawning gap between future mission obligations and available forces remains to be seen.

Schumpeter himself observed that innovation is driven by an entrepreneurial spirit and guided only by intuition.[12] New capabilities involve a step into an unknown where the knowledge of costs and benefits is murky at best. With respect to novel technologies, organisational structures and operational concepts, the military lacks the benefit of hindsight obtained by the audit of war and combat experience. Discarding traditional ways of war is risky because they are battle-tested solutions to operational challenges. Military officers may resist change out of a mistaken commitment to an outmoded capability or misplaced sentiment, but they can also insist on the continued relevance of current ways of war because of practical military wisdom. Historians of science and technology Andrew Russell and Lee Vinsel characterise this tendency as 'maintenance'.[13] The relentless pursuit of the next big thing – the driving force behind Silicon Valley start-ups – often neglects the important but less exciting work of straightforward upkeep.[14] Whether a given legacy capability should be actively maintained or has truly reached its expiration date is usually a matter of fierce and extended debate.

For innovation to be worthwhile, its marginal benefits for combat performance must exceed the marginal cost that stems from scotching legacy platforms, familiar concepts of operation and traditional organisational structures. This logic informs the popular but contested idea of 'divest to invest' that is prominent in today's defence-policy discussions. To modernise the force without significant increases in defence spending, the US armed services must consider what to retire to free up resources to purchase new capabilities. The air force plans to retire ageing fighters and bombers, and recapitalise with F-35s, B-21s, F-15EXs and Next Generation Air Dominance Fighters.[15] The navy's budget requests similarly follow a divest-to-invest approach that would decommission warships, such as the Littoral Combat Ship, before they reach their expected service lives to fund newer capabilities and platforms.[16] The Marine Corps has divested of legacy programmes to invest in systems that support the service's plan to refocus its capabilities on great-power conflict and operating inside an adversary's defensive bubble.[17]

These innovation efforts are not without risk. Resources saved must be invested in new capabilities and concepts that work reliably and facilitate missions that the services may eventually be called upon to accomplish. When the US Air Force became an independent service in 1947, it quickly latched onto the nuclear mission as its *raison d'être*. Nuclear weapons were seen as allowing air forces to accomplish what they failed to do in the Second World War – deliver rapid and decisive victory by obliterating the enemy's industrial centres. The air force thus cannibalised its close-air-support and air-superiority competencies to invest heavily in long-range nuclear-bombing capabilities.[18] Come the Korean War, however, US presidents did not authorise the air force to use nuclear weapons. The air force destroyed North Korea's industrial capacity, but the country did not capitulate. What the air force actually needed to be effective in its assigned missions were precisely its neglected capabilities: close air support for ground troops, fighter escorts for its bombers and air-to-air combat capabilities.[19]

This is not to say that a divest-to-invest approach is inherently flawed. There is no specific balance of creation and destruction that is ideal for all circumstances. Some platforms are indeed obsolete or irrelevant for the future fight. Some skill sets have become less suitable. Some missions are less likely than others. Therefore, calculated risks must be taken. Risks are heightened, however, when they are taken in desperation or out of a false sense of certainty about a coming revolution.

Necessity is the mother of risky innovation

Militaries are more likely to innovate when resources are scarce or threats are near, yet innovation is often expensive and takes time. When money and personnel are limited, military organisations need to find inventive ways to stretch what they have to cover more mission areas. One service might also innovate to compete with a rival service for a larger slice of the budgetary pie.[20] As armed conflict becomes more likely, professional military officers feel pressured to quickly devise new means and methods that better prepare the armed forces to fulfil national objectives.[21]

Stress-testing new war-fighting concepts, experimental units, and novel technologies and platforms in realistic environments can be expensive and place heavy demands on military personnel and equipment that reduce combat readiness. This reality is particularly problematic as the cost of weapons systems rises alongside their growing complexity and sophistication.[22] The British Army pioneered tank warfare in the First World War, but after the war lacked the resources necessary to realistically test the operational potential of its tanks. The cost of a single experimental medium tank could exceed the annual budget for tank trials.[23] The cost of weapons systems has ballooned. Take, for instance, missile defence. Engineering models alone cannot accurately predict how interceptors will be affected by various conditions, but the Missile Defense Agency's flight tests in real-world-like scenarios have consistently failed to meet schedules, in part to due to intercept-purchase delays.[24]

As international crises multiply and the security environment deteriorates, militaries can also feel the need to accelerate the innovation process. But some of the most successful military-innovation programmes involved decades of experimentation and debate. The development of German armoured warfare and US carrier warfare – canonical cases of military innovation – were protracted efforts that lasted from the First World War through the interwar period and into the Second World War.

Thomas Hughes coined the term 'reverse salient' to describe components of technological systems that underperform and hinder the system's overall development and performance.[25] To identify, assess and eliminate such problems involves time, attention, experience and familiarity. Rushing ahead invites trouble down the road. The US Navy's newest *Ford*-class aircraft carrier is several years behind its life cycle, significantly over budget and plagued by malfunctioning components. Admiral Michael Gilday, then chief of Naval Operations, admitted in July 2021 that the navy had been wrong to cram 23 new technologies into the new carrier. In the future, he warned, a more deliberate and constrained approach to introducing new technologies to a given platform will be needed.[26]

Without properly resourced experimentation and adequate time, military integration of novel technologies and concepts is likely to be slipshod. Embracing relatively untested capabilities drives up risk because there is a greater likelihood that they will ultimately fail or prove unreliable. In that case, the new capabilities are unlikely to offset the loss of traditional ones.

The once and future revolution

Militaries are more likely to innovate when there is a compelling vision of future warfare. But the more popular a proposal, the more ambitious its claims tend to be. It captures the imagination because it resonates with the way officers believe the world works or buttresses a given service's relevance or pre-eminence for the next major conflict. Innovators often make simplifying assumptions about the future combat environment and derive elegant holistic – and therefore seductive – solutions to operational challenges. These are not necessarily cynical ploys to secure resources. A hallmark of wishful thinking is the fanciful notion that all good things come together.[27]

Military organisations may be conservative overall, but military theorists are prone to indulge in misleading futurology.[28] Early air-power advocates prophesied a new era of warfare in which long-range aircraft armed with bombs would make naval vessels and large armies obsolete. Strategic bombing would directly attack the enemy's war-making capacity and bring wars to a rapid conclusion. The Second World War invalidated the more extreme versions of this vision.[29] After the Korean War, champions of tactical nuclear warfare proposed that in an age of nuclear plenty the army should trade mass for mobility. The army restructured field formations into austere combat divisions, labelled 'pentomic' for their five self-contained and highly mobile battlegroups. By operating in a dispersed fashion, a pentomic division could in theory evade Soviet nuclear targeting and use its own nuclear weapons against concentrations of enemy ground forces. The requisite leap-ahead technologies in firepower, mobility and communications never came to fruition. Exercises convinced army officers that dispersal was no answer to Soviet tactical nuclear weapons. The army eventually abandoned the concept and reverted to more traditional technologies, force structure and doctrine.[30]

The 'Revolution in Military Affairs' that mesmerised the US military establishment in the 1990s followed a similar pattern.[31] The Soviet-termed 'reconnaissance-strike complex' would produce wholesale increases in precision involving networked sensors to rapidly find, target and strike enemy assets. The US Air Force, Navy and Army each innovated in distinct ways but were guided by similar intuitions. Improvements in computers and electronics paved the way for long-range precision strike. Land vehicles, ships, missiles and aircraft had to become lighter, faster and stealthier for effective and efficient force projection. As sensor technologies steeply advanced, the battlefield would become 'transparent', and the key to victory became 'information dominance'. The revolution promised an economically sustainable form of warfare that would be fast and decisive, result in low casualties and apply to a range of contingencies. This revolution never arrived.

Yet all the prognostications had an element of validity. Strategic bombing made an important contribution to Allied victory in the Second World War. Tactical nuclear weapons remained a part of NATO's deterrence posture in Europe. Sensors and precision-guided munitions have in fact profoundly changed the way the United States wages war. But an element of fantasy had exaggerated the possibilities and wished away technical challenges, enemy countermeasures and political constraints that ultimately dashed the loftiest aspirations of military innovators.

Navigating innovation dilemmas

Some bets on innovation are better informed and more prudent than other ones. Three guiding principles can improve the quality of the process.

Firstly, drastic changes are intensely and inherently risky. History books often showcase mavericks, rule-breakers and iconoclasts, and some portray military innovators who disrupted the system as heroes who broke through a hidebound and conservative bureaucracy, even though wholesale adoption of their ideas might have been grossly irresponsible. Conversely, opponents of disruptive innovations are frequently cast as close-minded or reactionary naysayers, or, worse, cultic followers of outmoded ideas or technologies, even when their scepticism was prudent. It is an enduring shibboleth that generals are surprised in battle because they focus too much on refighting the last war. They can also neglect the lessons of recent combat experiences. Fixated on new technologies and corresponding proclamations of a new era of warfare, some military leaders may immerse themselves in preparing for a future war that never materialises, only to find themselves fighting an actual war that requires old capabilities. To curb this tendency, correcting the legends built around celebrated military officers who were fanatically committed to radical new ways of war would be salutary.[32]

The idea of disruptive innovation can, of course, sound appealing in part because there have been instances in which new technologies or methods have fundamentally changed the character of war to the benefit of the innovator. But these have been rare. Militaries tend to improve their performance through evolution as opposed to revolution, by sustaining rather than disrupting.[33] The Russia–Ukraine war reinforces this view. Some things have changed, but much remains the same. More futuristic visions of warfare have not been realised.[34] The newer domains of cyber and space are important but have not yet proven decisive. Drones receive the bulk of media attention, but tanks and artillery are still the most useful tools on the battlefield. Dumb artillery rounds likely account for the greatest casualty numbers and may end up being a significant, if not decisive, factor in the war's outcome.[35]

Secondly, beware of wishful thinking that exaggerates the impact of new capabilities and downplays enemy countermeasures, political ramifications and untested aspects of underlying technologies. The risks associated with major twentieth-century efforts to innovate were not lurking in the shadows. Sceptics publicly criticised well-known problems. Nevertheless, British armour innovators expected tanks to manoeuvre around enemy defences, which proved impossible in the Second World War when British units confronted German anti-tank guns in the deserts of North Africa. In the Korean War, the nuclear-fixated air force was called upon to wage war below the nuclear threshold. The technologies required to realise the army's pentomic vision never materialised. Seemingly comprehensive technical solutions often fail when faced with operational challenges.

Finally, although methodical and deliberate development of new weapons and concepts is slower, it reduces costly errors in producing and deploying new capabilities at scale. In contrast, bypassing rigorous vetting procedures in favour of rapid and dramatic reforms tends to obscure downside risks, particularly in complex organisations with multiple stakeholders.

In this vein, compare two US Army programmes, one an expensive blunder and the other a success that continues to pay dividends. While fighting in Afghanistan and Iraq, the army invested enormous amounts of time and resources into its multi-billion-dollar Future Combat Systems (FCS) programme – its primary modernisation effort in the 2000s, meant to radically transform its way of war by creating a whole new family of mobile ground vehicles networked together by an advanced communications architecture. It involved multiple unproven technologies that were arguably, like the service's earlier pentomic misadventure, nowhere close to reaching maturity.[36] In 2009, after massive cost overruns and insufficient technological advances, the Pentagon announced its cancellation. The programme produced only a few new capabilities. The army's High Mobility Artillery Rocket System (HIMARS), on the other hand, integrated proven technologies. After seeing action in Afghanistan and Syria, HIMARS became famous for its strong, though not decisive, contribution to Ukraine's performance in the Russia–Ukraine war.

*   *   *

Getting massive hierarchical bureaucracies such as the US armed services to change the way they do business is hard.[37] But even cautious brass have been more open to innovation than popular myth would have it. Cavalry generals were not, in fact, fanatically opposed to mechanisation via the tank.[38] Battleship admirals in the United States and Britain were not allergic to carrier warfare and experimented in peacetime with every aspect of naval aviation that came to the fore in the Pacific War.[39] The tugs-of-war between innovators and conservatives – a better term might be conservators or maintainers – were primarily about the pace of change and whether a new way of war had proven itself to the extent that the military could prudently let go of older means and methods.

Today, US military officers, defence analysts and policymakers broadly agree that innovation is necessary to compete with great-power rivals, and that it can provide the needed advantages to win the next major conflict. What is less clear is how to innovate and in what direction – which technologies, what kinds of reorganisation and which concepts of operation will be most effective against future enemies and in new combat environments. Service leaders and civilian policymakers will need to carefully weigh the risks, interrogate proposed solutions, monitor signs of wishful thinking, ensure that development processes include rigorous vetting procedures, and heed any audits of war that are available. It's safe to say that there are no panaceas.

Notes

[1] See, for example, Andrew F. Krepinevich, Jr, *The Origins of Victory: How Disruptive Military Innovation Determines the Fates of Great Powers* (New Haven, CT: Yale University Press, 2023).

[2] See Kendrick Kuo, 'Dangerous Changes: When Military Innovation Harms Combat Effectiveness', *International Security*, vol. 47, no. 2, Fall 2022, pp. 46–87.

[3] See Robert G. Angevine, 'Adapting to Disruption: Aerial Combat over North Vietnam', *Joint Forces Quarterly*, no. 96, 1st quarter 2020, pp. 74–83, esp. 76–7.

[4] See Joseph Schumpeter, *Capitalism, Socialism and Democracy*, 3rd edition (New York: Harper Perennial, 2008), p. 83.

[5] On defining military innovation, see Adam Grissom, 'The Future of Military Innovation Studies', *Journal of Strategic Studies*, vol. 29, no. 5, October

2006, pp. 905–34; and Michael C. Horowitz and Shira Pindyck, 'What Is a Military Innovation and Why It Matters', *Journal of Strategic Studies*, vol. 46, no. 1, March 2022, pp. 85–104.

[6] See US Department of Defense, 'Military and Security Developments Involving the People's Republic of China', Annual Report to Congress, 2023, pp. 164–72, https://media.defense. gov/2023/Oct/19/2003323409/-1/- 1/1/2023-MILITARY-AND-SECURITY- DEVELOPMENTS-INVOLVING-THE- PEOPLES-REPUBLIC-OF-CHINA.PDF.

[7] See John R. Hoehn, Kelley M. Sayler and Michael E. DeVine, 'Unmanned Aircraft Systems: Roles, Missions, and Future Concepts', CRS Report R47188, Congressional Research Service, 2022, pp. 6, 14–15.

[8] See US Air Force, 'Agile Combat Employment', Doctrine Note 1-21, 1 December 2021, https://www.af.mil/

Portals/1/documents/Force%20
Management/AFDN_1-21_ACE.pdf.

9   See Ronald O'Rourke, 'Navy Large
    Unmanned Surface and Undersea
    Vehicles: Background and Issues
    for Congress', CRS Report R45757,
    Congressional Research Service, 2023,
    pp. 20–7.

10 See Andrew Feickert, 'The Army's
    Multi-domain Task Force (MDTF)',
    CRS In Focus IF11797, Congressional
    Research Service, 2023.

11 See Andrew Feickert, 'U.S. Marine
    Corps Force Design 2030 Initiative:
    Background and Issues for Congress',
    CRS Report R47614, Congressional
    Research Service, 2023.

12 See Schumpeter, *Capitalism, Socialism
    and Democracy*, p. 132.

13 Andrew L. Russell and Lee
    Vinsel, 'After Innovation, Turn
    to Maintenance', *Technology and
    Culture*, vol. 59, no. 1, January 2018,
    pp. 1–25.

14 See Lee Vinsel and Andrew L. Russell,
    *The Innovation Delusion: How Our
    Obsession with the New Has Disrupted
    the Work that Matters Most* (New York:
    Crown Currency, 2020), pp. 11–12.

15 See Heather R. Penney, *The Future
    Fighter Force Our Nation Requires:
    Building a Bridge* (Arlington, VA:
    Mitchell Institute for Aerospace
    Studies, 2022), pp. 1–6.

16 See Office of the Chief of Naval
    Operations, 'Report to Congress
    on the Annual Long-range Plan
    for Construction of Naval Vessels
    for Fiscal Year 2023', April 2022,
    https://media.defense.gov/2022/
    Apr/20/2002980535/-1/-1/0/PB23%20
    SHIPBUILDING%20PLAN%2018%20
    APR%202022%20FINAL.PDF.

17 See Feickert, 'US Marine Corps Force
    Design 2030 Initiative', pp. 1–4.

18 See Thomas Alexander Hughes,
    *Overlord: General Pete Quesada and the
    Triumph of Tactical Air Power in World
    War II* (New York: Free Press, 1995),
    p. 312; and Phillip S. Meilinger, *Hoyt
    S. Vandenberg: The Life of a General*
    (Bloomington, IN: Indiana University
    Press, 1989), pp. 168–9.

19 See Thomas C. Hone, 'Korea', in
    Benjamin F. Cooling (ed.), *Case Studies
    in the Achievement of Air Superiority*
    (Washington DC: Center for Air
    Force History, 1994), pp. 453–504;
    Allan R. Millett, 'Korea, 1950–1953',
    in Benjamin Franklin Cooling (ed.),
    *Case Studies in the Development of Close
    Air Support* (Washington DC: US
    Government Printing Office, 1990),
    pp. 345–410; and Wayne Thompson,
    'The Air War Over Korea', in Bernard
    C. Nalty (ed.), *Winged Shield, Winged
    Sword: A History of the United States Air
    Force*, Volume II (Washington DC: Air
    Force History and Museums Program,
    1997), pp. 3–52.

20 See Owen Reid Cote, Jr, *The Politics of
    Innovative Military Doctrine: The U.S.
    Navy and Fleet Ballistic Missiles*, PhD
    dissertation, Massachusetts Institute of
    Technology, 1996, pp. 339–42.

21 See Barry R. Posen, *The Sources of
    Military Doctrine: France, Britain,
    and Germany Between the World Wars*
    (Ithaca, NY: Cornell University Press,
    1984), pp. 59, 74–5.

22 See John A. Alic, *Trillions for Military
    Technology: How the Pentagon Innovates
    and Why It Costs So Much* (New York:
    Palgrave Macmillan, 2007), pp. 49–106.

23 See J.P. Harris, 'British Armour and
    Rearmament in the 1930s', *Journal of*

Strategic Studies, vol. 11, no. 2, 1988, pp. 220–44.

24 See Ronald O'Rourke, 'Navy Aegis Ballistic Missile Defense (BMD) Program: Background and Issues for Congress', CRS Report RL33745, Congressional Research Service, 2023, pp. 26–9.

25 Thomas P. Hughes, 'The Evolution of Large Technological Systems', in Wiebe E. Bijker, Thomas P. Hughes and Trevor Pinch (eds) *The Social Construction of Technological Systems: New Directions in the Sociology and History of Technology* (Cambridge, MA: MIT Press, 1987), pp. 73–6.

26 See Justin Katz, 'CNO: Too Much New Tech on Ford Was a Mistake', *Breaking Defense*, 21 July 2021, https://breakingdefense.com/2021/07/cno-too-much-new-tech-on-ford-was-a-mistake/.

27 See Bent Flyvbjerg and Cass R. Sunstein, 'The Principle of the Malevolent Hiding Hand; or, the Planning Fallacy Writ Large', *Social Research*, vol. 83, no. 4, Winter 2016, pp. 979–1,004.

28 See Lawrence Freedman, *The Future of War: A History* (New York: PublicAffairs, 2019), pp. 264–87.

29 See Mark Clodfelter, 'Molding Airpower Convictions: Development and Legacy of William Mitchell's Strategic Thought', in Phillip S. Meilinger (ed.), *The Paths of Heaven: The Evolution of Airpower Theory* (Maxwell Air Force Base, AL: Air University Press, 1997), pp. 79–114.

30 On the pentomic army, see Andrew J. Bacevich, *The Pentomic Era: The U.S. Army Between Korea and Vietnam* (Washington DC: National Defense

University Press, 1986); and Brian McAllister Linn, *Elvis's Army: Cold War GIs and the Atomic Battlefield* (Cambridge, MA: Harvard University Press, 2016).

31 On the Revolution in Military Affairs, see Lawrence Freedman, *The Revolution in Strategic Affairs* (London: Routledge for the IISS, 1998); and Elinor C. Sloan, *The Revolution in Military Affairs* (Kingston: McGill-Queen's University Press, 2002).

32 For an example of demythologising pertaining to American manoeuvre-warfare maven John Boyd, see Stephen Robinson, *The Blind Strategist: John Boyd and the American Art of War* (Dunedin: Exisle Publishing, 2021).

33 See Andrew L. Ross. 'On Military Innovation: Toward an Analytical Framework', Study of Innovation and Technology in China, Policy Brief no. 1, September 2010, p. 2, https://escholarship.org/uc/item/3d0795p8.

34 See Stephen Biddle, 'Back in the Trenches: Why New Technology Hasn't Revolutionized Warfare in Ukraine', *Foreign Affairs*, vol. 102, no. 5, September/October 2023, pp. 153–64; and Franz-Stefan Gady and Michael Kofman, 'Ukraine's Strategy of Attrition', *Survival*, vol. 65, no. 2, April–May 2023, pp. 7–22.

35 See David Johnson, 'The Army Risks Reasoning Backwards in Analyzing Ukraine', *War on the Rocks*, 14 June 2022, https://warontherocks.com/2022/06/the-army-risks-reasoning-backwards-in-analyzing-ukraine/; and Gady and Kofman, 'Ukraine's Strategy of Attrition', pp. 7–8.

36 See Government Accountability Office, 'Defense Acquisitions: Key

Decisions to Be Made on Future Combat System', GAO-07-376, 2007, pp. 13–16, https://www.gao.gov/assets/gao-07-376.pdf.

37 See David Barno and Nora Bensahel, *Adaptation Under Fire: How Militaries Change in Wartime* (New York: Oxford University Press, 2020), pp. 10–17.

38 See David French, 'The Mechanization of the British Cavalry Between the World Wars', *War in History*, vol. 10, no. 3, July 2003, pp. 296–320; and Robin Prior and Trevor Wilson, *Command on the Western Front: The Military Career of Sir Henry Rawlinson 1914–18* (Oxford: Blackwell, 1992), pp. 292–5, 311–15.

39 See Kendrick Kuo, 'Military Innovation and Technological Determinism: British and US Ways of Carrier Warfare, 1919–1945', *Journal of Global Security Studies*, vol. 6, no. 3, September 2021, pp. 1–19.

The Green Transition and European Industry

Nicholas Crawford

The transition from fossil fuels to renewable energy opens new areas of economic and geopolitical competition.[1] Advanced economies are competing to lead in manufacturing clean technologies, and other countries with the mineral resources needed for those technologies are growing in strategic importance.[2] At the same time, the energy transition has geostrategic implications for the industries that use the 'clean energy' these technologies produce, particularly those that use a lot of it. For energy-intensive industries, geography still matters. A solar or wind farm produces very different amounts of energy in different parts of the world. Clean-energy costs will be correspondingly uneven.

Mainly in the nineteenth century, Europe gave birth to many energy-intensive industries that remain critical to the global economy. The steel and chemicals industries were central to the emergence of various industrial hubs across Western Europe.[3] The region is now spearheading efforts to decarbonise both traditional energy-intensive industries and sectors such as shipping and aviation. But owing to Western Europe's geography – its climate, population density and level of economic development – it faces an uphill struggle to retain its energy-intensive industries. Clean energy will be much more expensive in Europe's industrial heartlands than in other parts of

Nicholas Crawford is a systemic- and emerging-risk expert at Euroclear. The views expressed in this article are the author's and not those of Euroclear.

Survival | vol. 66 no. 1 | February–March 2024 | pp. 99–124   https://doi.org/10.1080/00396338.2024.2309078

the world, and using the continent's clean energy to power energy-intensive industries will push up costs for other energy users. European governments plan to decarbonise some industries by importing green hydrogen and its derivatives from countries with cheaper renewables. But it looks increasingly likely that some of these industries will relocate to the source of cheap green hydrogen, rather than importing it into Europe.

Europe therefore faces major dislocations in some energy-intensive industries. This reality flies in the face of the current deglobalisation trend. While European governments will instinctively want to intervene to prop up these industries and encourage investment in future energy-intensive industries in Europe, the strategic case for doing so is weak.

Europe's energy problems

The energy crisis that beset Europe following Russia's 2022 invasion of Ukraine was a wake-up call for the region's energy-intensive industries. They warned that high energy prices could be 'life-threatening' and an 'existential threat', leading to a 'breaking point' for key parts of Europe's economy.[4] Belgium's prime minister, among others, cautioned that the region faced imminent deindustrialisation.[5] Although industry representatives' dire warnings should be treated cautiously, theirs was not an idle concern. Europe's aluminium production fell by 12.5% and halted altogether at several plants.[6] Steel production sank to peak-pandemic 2020 levels.[7] BASF, the world's largest chemicals company, shuttered one of its German plants.[8]

Energy prices in Europe have since fallen, and although natural gas is never likely to be as cheap in the region as it once was, the immediate threat of deindustrialisation appears to have passed. European governments have also made generous efforts to dampen the energy-cost pressures on industry. Under the terms of the European Union's 'Temporary Crisis Framework for State Aid', Germany alone announced €99 billion in gas and electricity subsidies for just a 15-month period, though with falling gas and electricity prices it is on track to spend less than half the planned amount.[9]

There remain medium-term concerns in Europe about the economic risks of reducing greenhouse-gas emissions faster than in other parts of the world. Imports from countries that reduce emissions more slowly could undercut European businesses on price. Alternatively, European businesses may move their emissions-intensive activities outside Europe, causing 'carbon leakage'. As a result, the EU has introduced its controversial Carbon Border Adjustment Mechanism (CBAM), which imposes a tariff on select goods arriving in the EU from countries with lower or no carbon pricing. With most countries aspiring to transition to clean energy, this competition between European products made with renewables and imports made with fossil fuels should be a temporary concern.

Looking 15–20 years ahead, however, when energy-intensive goods and services will be produced with clean energy around the world, Europe will face a new challenge against which CBAM offers no protection. As an unavoidable result of the region's geography, Europe will have an absolute and comparative disadvantage in renewable energy, especially in the traditional industrial heartlands of Western Europe.

Western Europe has a mild climate and high land prices, which makes solar and onshore-wind generation more costly per unit of energy than in many other parts of the world. Electricity from onshore-wind projects in Brazil, Canada, China, India, Spain and the United States is almost a third cheaper than in France and the United Kingdom, and 50% cheaper than in Germany. Electricity from large-scale solar generation in countries like China and Australia is between one-half and two-thirds the cost of solar in Germany.[10] And even the most efficient hydropower plant in Europe produces electricity at a cost 80% higher than that of the most efficient hydropower plant in Asia.[11] Moreover, in densely populated Western Europe, the opportunity cost of using renewable energy in energy-intensive industries is much higher than elsewhere. Western Europe has twice the land mass of Texas but nine times the population, and renewable energy is currently two to three times more expensive in Western Europe than in Texas.[12]

That clean energy is expensive in Europe is not news. The European Commission and the Belgian, Dutch and German governments have acknowledged, for example, that the high cost of renewables means that Western Europe cannot affordably produce enough green hydrogen, which is produced by splitting water into hydrogen and oxygen in a renewable-energy-powered electrolyser, and is needed to decarbonise key industries. Not only will it be cheaper to produce that green hydrogen where renewable energy is cheaper, but the volumes of hydrogen required mean that a huge amount of land would be needed for solar panels and wind farms. The green-transition strategies of the EU, Germany and others are therefore premised on importing the majority of their green hydrogen and hydrogen derivatives from countries that can produce it much more cheaply.

Europe's energy-intensive industries face an even bigger problem owing to the confluence of three economic realities. Firstly, the impact of high renewable-electricity prices is more significant than it appeared to be prior to the energy crisis of 2022. Secondly, transmitting electricity and transporting green hydrogen over long distances are likely to be prohibitively expensive. Thirdly, energy-intensive industries in Western Europe will confront infrastructure bottlenecks and local opposition. If companies – especially those producing basic metals and commodity chemicals, but also some downstream manufacturers – continue to operate in Western Europe, they are likely to be undercut by cheap green imports.

The upshot is that some energy-intensive industries are likely to relocate overseas to places where renewables are available at much lower cost. While other big users of electricity, such as data centres and greenhouses, probably will not leave Europe, their growth in the region may be stymied. Emerging industries such as e-methanol, synthetic aviation fuel and direct air capture of carbon dioxide are unlikely to take root in Western Europe. There are mitigating factors. Building new plants overseas is expensive, the cost of capital in Western Europe is low compared to other regions, and producing goods close to the large European market has commercial advantages. Europe could also benefit from technological advances in renewables generation and hydrogen shipping, or from drilling underground hydrogen reservoirs like those in France and Spain. But such developments remain a distant prospect. Modelling indicates that for some major industries – even with optimistic assumptions for current technologies – Europe's advantages do not offset the disadvantages.[13]

Germany, which hosts much of Europe's energy-intensive industry, is just starting to grapple with the scale of this challenge. Discussions are under way within the chancellery, economy ministry and finance ministry about the prospect of Germany losing its comparative advantage in energy-intensive industries and what the government should do about it.[14] The main measure under debate is the economy ministry's proposal for a big electricity subsidy for energy-intensive industries.[15] The German government is also revisiting its long-standing opposition to carbon capture and storage in recognition of the role it could play in reducing emissions from energy-intensive industries without immediately switching to renewable electricity or clean hydrogen.[16]

Drivers of industrial relocation

High clean-energy costs will not be fatal for all Europe's industries – not even for all its energy-intensive ones. But among the European industries that are vulnerable to dislocation, each in different ways, are steel, various chemicals, aluminium, data centres, indoor horticulture and future clean fuels.

Steel

Primary-steel production involves processing iron ore into steel, traditionally in a coal- or gas-fired blast furnace, and is a major energy-intensive industry.[17] Decarbonising primary-steel production will require large amounts of clean hydrogen and brand-new integrated steel plants. Europe currently has primary-steel production capacity of 98 million tonnes per year, excluding Turkiye and Ukraine.[18] New plants currently cost roughly $1bn per million tonnes of annual output.[19] Thus, the initial investment cost of replacing all Europe's primary plants with green-hydrogen power plants is around $100bn, though as green-steel production matures plant costs are likely to fall.[20]

Renewable-energy costs have a significant impact on the cost of green steel, primarily due to the cost of green hydrogen. According to one study, every additional $10 per megawatt hour of energy adds more than $30 per tonne to the cost of green steel.[21] Crucially, it is cheaper to transport steel products than it is to transport the green hydrogen and iron ore required to produce them. Labour costs are often lower outside Western Europe as well. Accordingly, there is a strong economic case for relocating primary-steel production away from its traditional hubs in Western Europe to countries which have, in close proximity, both large commercial-grade iron-ore reserves and the potential to produce cheap green hydrogen. The strongest candidates are likely to be Australia and Brazil.[22] One study has shown that even in Sweden, which has commercial-grade iron ore and among the cheapest renewables in Europe, projected green-steel production costs will be around 40% higher than in Brazil throughout 2030–50.[23]

Commodity chemicals

The largest of the chemical industries facing geographic dislocation is ammonia, the market for which is currently worth around $80bn annually, with the EU accounting for 8% of production.[24] However, the market could increase in size from 185m to more than 550m tonnes by 2050, driven by demand for ammonia as a shipping fuel and as a fuel for power generation.[25] Shipping is likely to be the main driver of increased demand in Europe. Decarbonising ammonia production involves using green hydrogen in place of natural gas, with energy and green hydrogen accounting for more than 50% of the production cost of green ammonia. Therefore, Europe is expected to have the highest average green-ammonia production costs of all major economic regions, around 67% higher than in the most favourable locations globally by 2040 at $500 per tonne compared to $300 per tonne.[26] Factoring in the cost of shipping, European businesses could save 25–30% on green ammonia by importing it from low-cost production locations.[27] A prominent example is Oman, which has already agreed to land leases for three large-scale green-ammonia projects, led respectively by the United Kingdom's BP and Shell and South Korea's POSCO. Saudi Arabia also expects to export large volumes of ammonia from its planned plant in Neom. In addition, Australia, Egypt and Namibia will probably export green ammonia, and may see large inorganic-chemical and agrichemical industries spring up as well.

The green-hydrogen industry also has by-products that may induce other commodity-chemical industries to relocate. Many green-hydrogen plants will use desalinated water, leaving brine as a by-product. The chlor-alkali industry electrolyses brine to produce chlorine and caustic soda. Not only is it worth around $65bn globally, but it is essential for production of many other chemicals.[28] In Europe, 55% of all chemical production relies on outputs of the chlor-alkali industry.[29] Europe currently has 62 chlor-alkali plants across 19 countries, with Germany accounting for about 45% of production.[30] Electricity accounts for around half of the production costs and brine around 18%.[31] Further processes are employed to produce hydrochloric acid and vinyl chloride. Integrating with green-hydrogen production in coastal deserts would provide chlor-alkali outfits with low-cost renewable energy and by-product brine, plus the infrastructure to handle the hydrogen it produces as a by-product. By 2050, green-hydrogen production is expected to reach 500m–680m tonnes, and if seawater is used for just half of this, the by-product brine would contain enough chlorine to meet current world demand.[32] Europe's chlor-alkali industry is unlikely to disappear overnight as billions of dollars have been sunk into existing facilities. But chlor-alkali companies will likely target green-hydrogen clusters as part of their expansion plans, and, as existing European facilities age and are decommissioned, the region's chlor-alkali industry may shrink.

Aluminium

The outlook for Europe's aluminium industry is relatively straightforward. Energy typically accounts for around 40% of the production costs of primary aluminium, and a higher proportion as electricity costs rise.[33] In the wake of Russia's 2022 invasion of Ukraine, skyrocketing electricity prices in Europe boosted that component to 80% of production costs.[34] The region's production fell by 12.5%, halting altogether at one plant in Germany.[35] This came in the wake of a protracted decline in European production, from 4.6m tonnes in 2008 to 2.9m in 2022, against regional demand of 5m.[36] The global aluminium market is the second-most valuable metals market after gold, worth around $160bn–170bn each year, and aluminium demand is expected to grow 40% by 2030 due to the metal's criticality to the energy transition.[37]

Green-aluminium production requires a huge, uninterrupted supply of clean electricity. Currently, 61% of the power to aluminium smelters in Europe comes from hydropower, 13% from other renewables, 10% from coal, 9% from nuclear and 5% from other fossil fuels. Scandinavia accounts for most of the region's aluminium production because of its abundance in hydropower. Iceland, using geothermal energy, is a notable producer too. Germany, Greece and Spain rely more heavily on a combination of fossil fuels and variable renewables. With poor hydropower and geothermal resources, they will be uncompetitive in the production of green aluminium. The outlook for France, which has Europe's single-largest aluminium smelter, in Dunkirk, and powers it with expensive nuclear energy, is less clear. But it is safe to say that, other things being equal, European producers without access to cheap hydropower or geothermal energy will struggle to survive the energy transition, losing out to countries expected to add the most new hydropower capacity, including Brazil, China, India, Vietnam and other Latin American and Southeast Asian countries despite local opposition.

Data centres

Another energy-intensive economic sector is data centres, which are expected to account for 3.2% of Europe's electricity consumption by 2030.[38] In some European countries, the share is much higher; in Ireland, data centres consumed 17% of all electricity in 2021 and will consume 27% by 2030.[39] The technology company Meta recently proposed the construction of a hyperscale data centre in the Netherlands that would have consumed 1.38 terawatt hours of electricity annually, or 6% of the country's current renewables generation.[40] Its plan was to use locally generated wind energy and to draw on local canals for its water-cooling system. This would either place significant additional demand on the Netherlands' electricity grid or require Meta to build around 500 megawatts of dedicated wind capacity plus batteries – the equivalent of the country's largest existing onshore wind farm and requiring upwards of 80 square kilometres of land.[41] Faced with local opposition and a government environmental review, Meta shelved its plans.[42]

In general, governments are increasingly reluctant to grant grid connections to data centres due to the strain they place on their electricity networks. In the densely populated, energy-thirsty countries of Western Europe, there are many competing electricity demands. In 2022, Ireland imposed a moratorium on new data centres until 2028.[43] The Netherlands introduced strict restrictions on the construction of any new facilities.[44] The EU requires much of the data collected within the bloc to remain on data servers in the region, which limits technology companies' ability to avoid bottlenecks by locating servers outside the EU. However, the EU does allow data flows to countries it recognises as having equivalent data-protection legislation. Among them are Argentina, Canada and the United States, which impose fewer obstacles to the installation of new, renewables-powered data centres.

Indoor horticulture

For the Netherlands, intensive indoor agriculture may present a major challenge for its electricity infrastructure. Globally, indoor agriculture is a $350bn industry, and the Netherlands has been a leader in its growth, having become the world's second-largest agricultural exporter despite its small land mass. However, climate-controlled and illuminated greenhouses and vertical farms currently account for 11% of the Netherlands' electricity use. As with data centres, energy makes up just a small share – 8–10% – of the production costs of greenhouse agriculture.[45] While intensive indoor agriculture is unlikely to relocate in search of the lowest-cost energy, any limits on new grid connections for new greenhouse farms could hinder the continued growth of the industry in Europe.

New energy-intensive industries

High clean-energy costs also mean that emerging energy-intensive industries are unlikely to flourish in Western Europe. Synthetic aviation fuel is currently the most promising option for decarbonising aviation. In 2022, the aviation-fuel market was worth $250bn worldwide, with synthetic fuel constituting a growing share.[46] Likewise, e-methanol, alongside ammonia, is an important prospective shipping fuel. The Danish shipping giant Maersk has already commissioned several e-methanol-powered ships. Both synthetic aviation fuel and e-methanol rely on clean hydrogen and captured carbon dioxide, and as hydrogen is more expensive to transport than carbon dioxide, synthetic aviation fuel and e-methanol production will co-locate with green-hydrogen clusters.[47] Synthetic fuel exported to Europe from low-cost locations is expected to be 17–20% cheaper than locally produced fuel by 2030, with the cost advantage likely to grow through to 2050.[48] With less carbon dioxide required, even larger cost advantages are likely for e-methanol. Europe, then, is likely to lose out.

Finally, direct air capture will become a major industry. The International Energy Agency expects it to be used to neutralise around one gigatonne of carbon dioxide annually by 2050, or 2.7% of the world's 2022 emissions. Other estimates run as high as five or even ten gigatonnes.[49] Like green-hydrogen production, direct air capture is very energy- and land-intensive. Solar-powering the capture of one gigatonne of carbon dioxide would require 20,000 to 35,000 km^2 of land. Direct air capture also works best in cold, dry locations. Central Asia and northwestern regions of China, parts of the Andes, the inland west of the US, and areas of South Africa, North Africa, Spain and southern Australia are best suited.[50] Western Europe is likely to play only a marginal role.

The case for non-intervention

The West's loss of manufacturing activity to China, its shrinking technological edge, its dependence on China for many critical goods, and the competitive advantage Beijing affords Chinese manufacturers through generous subsidies have drastically changed Western economic policies. Efforts to reduce trade dependence on China and reshore a wide range of manufacturing industries have been central to the West's new policies and are shaping a new era of deglobalisation.[51] The energy transition has provided an additional pull in that direction by increasing regional and national competition for leadership in clean-energy technologies.

Energy-intensive industries that start relocating away from Europe will be swimming against the tide of deglobalisation, leaving Europe more reliant on international supply chains, including in defence-related industries. Furthermore, retaining heavy industry is often a matter of pride at both the national and the local level, as industries like steelmaking have constituted a core part of the identity of industrial communities and perceptions of their standing. Accordingly, there will be no shortage of voices in industry and politics stressing the strategic importance of energy-intensive industries and the thousands of jobs that could be lost in Europe were these industries to move overseas, and they will undoubtedly call on governments to step in with financial support worth tens of billions. But European governments should be very cautious about trying to prevent the relocation of energy-intensive industries.

Social and political impact

There are socio-economic reasons for allowing the relocation of energy-intensive industries away from Western Europe (and, for that matter, Northeast Asia, which has an even less favourable energy landscape). Due to its climate, Europe needs much more land to generate the same amount of energy as other parts of the world. To conserve land and other resources, Europe needs to prioritise electricity for those industries that cannot easily move overseas. Further, although some affected companies would shift to other economically advanced areas – Australia, China, the Gulf and North America – others would move to developing economies, such as those in Latin America and North Africa, and substantially benefit them. Finally, within Europe, efforts to hold onto these industries would effectively force consumers to accept higher prices for energy or higher taxes to subsidise local production.

Furthermore, some dislocations may be merely intra-regional. Belgium, Germany, Italy, the Netherlands and the United Kingdom would be vulnerable, as they are densely populated and face intense competition for energy and land. But Finland, Norway and Sweden are less than one-eighth as densely populated, have excellent hydro- and wind-energy resources, and enjoy access to critical minerals close by.[52] Spain and Portugal are also less densely populated, and have good renewable resources. Thus, industrial dislocations could benefit some European states.

Moreover, many downstream activities will remain. In the steel industry, for instance, Western Europe will likely import semi-finished products, such as sponge iron or steel slab, as inputs for local production of finished, specialist steel goods. Already, Brazil and the United States have established this kind of arrangement, with global steel giant ArcelorMittal exporting primary-steel slab from its Brazilian plant to the United States for down-stream industrial uses.[53]

Although there are big differences between the affected energy-intensive industries, they are generally capital-intensive rather than labour-intensive. For example, the chemicals industry employs around 3m people in Europe, but few work in affected segments of the industry.[54] The chlor-alkali industry employs just 6,600 people directly and 39,000 indirectly across Europe. Of the roughly 85,000 employed in Europe's aluminium industry, just 20,000 are employed upstream in smelting, where energy costs cause the biggest problems. The rest are employed downstream in manufacturing finished products and recycling – activities that are more likely to remain in the region.[55] Even the steel industry employs few workers directly. Its 320,000 jobs across the EU account for less than 0.2% of the bloc's workforce.[56] And only a fraction of those jobs are in primary steelmaking, which will be hit hardest by the energy transition.[57]

The political impact could be much more significant. Employment in primary steelmaking, for example, is heavily concentrated in a few towns and cities. When a steel plant closes, local economies struggle to absorb the laid-off workers, and closures have a wider economic impact on the surrounding communities. The political pressure from these communities and labour unions to save jobs can create major problems for local and national politicians. This is one reason the steel industry regularly causes trade friction, as it recently did in talks between the United States and Europe.[58] Clearly, governments need to put plans in place to help single-industry towns transform their local economies by attracting alternative employers. But at an economy-wide level, it is more important to ensure that crude-steel costs are kept down and that the finished products remain competitive, as there are 80 downstream jobs for every one job in steelmaking itself.[59] The same goes for other energy-intensive industries. Three-quarters of aluminium-industry jobs are downstream, so ensuring cheap semi-finished aluminium is essential.

Governments have, of course, failed to effectively manage industrial dislocation before. China's 2001 entry into the World Trade Organization is widely blamed for the loss of manufacturing jobs in the West. And although the United States was affected much more severely than Europe, governments have been panned for their neo-liberal policies and failure to mitigate the local effects of globalisation.[60] However, dislocations in energy-intensive industries are of a much smaller order of magnitude and are therefore more manageable. Whereas the 'China shock' cut across vast swathes of manufacturing activity, affecting companies large and small in innumerable subsectors, the impact of high energy prices will affect a small number of large companies in a few, concentrated locations. This should make it more feasible for governments to attract companies to replace energy-intensive industries with new large-scale employers, such as factories for electric vehicles and the batteries that they use.

Strategic importance

Claims that the affected industries are strategically important also warrant close scrutiny. There is no doubt that it would be dangerous for Europe to rely wholly on, say, China for its supply of primary steel and aluminium, commodity chemicals, and shipping and aviation fuels. But to present the future of these industries in such stark terms – either produce in Europe or rely on China or another single country – is misleading and blinkered. It is more likely that European governments will work with the private sector to develop diversified, low-cost supply chains from a variety of partner countries.

One conspicuous reason the production of primary steel and primary aluminium is cast as strategically important is the role it plays in the defence industry.[61] In 2018, the Trump administration cited the importance of these metals to defence as its justification for introducing 25% and 10% tariffs on steel and aluminium, respectively, to protect the United States' domestic production of these metals. In theory, the loss of primary-steel and -aluminium production could leave defence industries vulnerable in the event of a major war that disrupted international shipping. In addition, the metals are essential for maintaining a just-in-time manufacturing capability in the automotive sector and other major industries. Events like the COVID-19 pandemic and the Suez Canal blockage of 2021 could play havoc with just-in-time industries if they rely heavily on long-distance supply chains for critical inputs.

Several considerations, however, dilute the strategic-value rationale for intervening in the primary-steel and -aluminium industries. For one, it is practically meaningless for Europe to prop up the primary-steel and -aluminium industries in anticipation of wartime disruption of international trade when it has little local mining of the main raw-material inputs for these industries – iron ore and bauxite. International trade in these products could equally be disrupted. In Europe, only Sweden and Ukraine mine significant quantities of iron ore for steel.[62] Norway is the region's leader in aluminium-ore production with a mere 2.3% of global production.[63] As of 2021, Germany imported around 70% of its iron ore and virtually all its aluminium ore from outside Europe.[64] Various other metals are required for alloying, and few of these are mined in Europe.[65]

Prospects for secondary steel (made from scrap) and secondary aluminium are also brighter in Europe. Although not all high-performance steel can currently be made purely from steel scrap, innovations in the industry may enable secondary steelmakers to produce higher grades of steel.[66] Already, advanced high-strength steels made from almost 100% scrap can satisfy many automotive and defence applications, such as shipbuilding.[67] Likewise, the future looks brighter for Europe's secondary-aluminium production than it does for its primary-aluminium production. In addition, primary steel and aluminium are unlikely to be imported as finished products straight into just-in-time industries.

Chemical industries vulnerable to energy-related dislocation do produce key inputs into a wide range of downstream industries in Europe – chlorine for producing plastics, medicines and water purification; and ammonia for fertilisers. But again, securing the downstream industries themselves is much more important. Ensuring that the pharmaceuticals industry, for instance, retains access to competitively priced inputs is crucial, whether they come from within Europe or outside its borders. That industry already imports a large share of its active ingredients from foreign shores, primarily China. Although in the wake of the COVID-19 pandemic the EU has tried to reduce dependence for them on China, a resilient supply chain could be ensured by geographic diversification, as well as reshoring.[68]

The questionable feasibility of industrial intervention

European governments – particularly Germany – might be able to prop up energy-intensive industries, but only at significant economic and political cost. And given the market distortions and political ruptures this would cause within the EU, it is doubtful that governments could intervene on a scale necessary to keep Europe's existing industrial hubs competitive.

The conventional approach to intervention in Europe is to subsidise the investment costs of adopting clean-energy technologies in affected industries. European governments and the EU have already announced billions of euros in subsidies of this kind for new green-steel plants and green-ammonia facilities. In many cases, however, capital costs account for only a small share of total production costs. For example, capital expenditure constitutes just 14% of green-steel production costs in competitive locations (around $60 per ton), meaning that, after investment subsidies, green steel produced in Western Europe will still be more than 20% more expensive than imports by 2050.[69] Furthermore, not all industries require new plants. Green-aluminium producers, for example, do not need to build new aluminium smelters.

An alternative is to subsidise the inputs to energy-intensive industries, namely electricity or green hydrogen. There are already some plans in place for input subsidies, but only as temporary measures to smooth the decarbonisation of key industries. The EU, Germany and the UK plan some form of temporary hydrogen subsidies to cover the difference between the market price for clean hydrogen and the price at which companies are willing and able to produce it. The German government is also debating the introduction of a controversial electricity subsidy for energy-intensive industries. To sustain Europe's energy-intensive industries in the long term, however, would require a more permanent regime of input subsidies, at immense cost. The proposed German electricity subsidy has been estimated at €4bn per year.[70] Likewise, the German government's ten-year subsidy for its green-steel plant in Duisburg, to cover the cost premium for green hydrogen over blue hydrogen, is almost three times the subsidy for capital expenditure on the plant.[71]

To put Germany's primary-steel industry on a competitive footing, Berlin would need to cover a large part of the cost difference between importing hydrogen for German steel production and importing steel made with cheaper hydrogen overseas. A back-of-the-envelope calculation suggests that, at Germany's current primary-steel output, the cost of such a subsidy could be as much as $3bn annually through 2050.[72] Output subsidies, or 'production credits', would be similarly expensive.

Unsurprisingly, measures like Germany's proposed electricity subsidy are controversial. There is no agreement among the governing coalition's parties on the measure, and most German economists oppose it. The European Commission has warned that it would drastically distort Europe's single market. Germany already accounts for 53% of the state aid distributed in Europe, and other EU members are concerned about the impact of still more German subsidies on non-German European companies.[73] Insofar as such subsidies might well run afoul of EU law, the European Commission and the EU General Court would likely strike them down.

*   *   *

In 2011, the World Energy Council framed an 'energy trilemma' whereby the world faced three competing energy-policy objectives: energy security (or autonomy), energy equity (or affordability) and environmental sustainability.[74] Today, the trade-offs are no longer clear-cut. Renewables are often cheaper than fossil fuels, making it easier to reconcile sustainability, affordability and security than it was a decade ago. But the challenges Europe faces from having comparatively high clean-energy costs have posed an emerging industrial trilemma. Industrial security, industrial efficiency and industrial sustainability come into conflict for energy-intensive industries. The problem is acute when industrial security is assumed to require domestic production or 'autonomy', which is the general thrust of the United States' and EU's deglobalisation policies.

The trade-offs are clear. Moving energy-intensive industries to places with comparative advantages in clean energy is the economically efficient option, but it comes at a cost in terms of industrial security. By contrast, keeping these energy-intensive industries in high-energy-cost locations means either subsidising these industries and sacrificing efficiency, or accepting the continued use of fossil fuels and contravening sustainability. It is easy to imagine Western European governments pledging to keep basic metals and chemicals production onshore, encouraging further investment into emerging energy-intensive industries, and wrangling over large financial packages to support investment in new clean-energy-fuelled plants and factories. The danger is that they will do so without a true sense of whether those subsidies will be sufficient to secure the industries' future in Europe, and that they will rely on a flimsy political and geostrategic case for propping these industries up.

Autonomy – essentially, the domestic production of goods – is not a guarantor of industrial security, particularly for energy-intensive industries that rely on a renewable-energy supply that could be disrupted by severe climatic and geological events. Unseasonably low rainfall can reduce availability of hydropower; volcanic-ash clouds can hamper solar generation; prolonged doldrums can cause periods of serious wind-power shortage. A diversity of cost-competitive suppliers in various regions is a more reliable way of minimising the risk of supply-chain disruption and ensuring that downstream industries in Europe remain strong. European governments can resolve the industrial trilemma by shaping diverse global supply chains for energy-intensive goods and mitigating the impact of dislocations in these industries on local economies.

Notes

[1] See Jason Bordoff and Meghan O'Sullivan, 'Green Upheaval: The New Geopolitics of Energy', *Foreign Affairs*, vol. 101, no. 1, January–February 2022, pp. 68–84; Daniel Scholten et al., 'The Geopolitics of Renewables: New Board, New Game', *Energy Policy*, vol. 138, art. 111059, March 2020; and Daniel Yergin, *The New Map: Energy, Climate, and the Clash of Nations* (New York: Penguin, 2020).

[2] See Lukasz Bednarski, *Lithium: The Global Race for Battery Dominance and* *the New Energy Revolution* (London: Hurst, 2021); Juan Pablo Medina Bickel and Irene Mia, 'Geopolitics and Climate Change: The Significance of South America', *Survival*, vol. 65, no. 4, August–September 2023, pp. 123–38; Guillaume Pitron, *The Rare Metals War: The Dark Side of Clean Energy and Digital Technologies* (London: Scribe, 2022); and Henry Sanderson, *Volt Rush: The Winners and Losers in the Race to Go Green* (London: Oneworld, 2023).

3   Western Europe here refers to Belgium, Denmark, France, Germany, Ireland, Luxembourg, the Netherlands, Switzerland and the United Kingdom.

4   See, respectively, EUROFER, 'Emergency EU Measures Immediately Needed to Overcome Life-threatening Energy Crisis for European Steel Industry', press release, 9 September 2022, https://www.eurofer.eu/press-releases/emergency-eu-measures-immediately-needed-to-overcome-life-threatening-energy-crisis-for-european-steel-industry/; Eurometaux, 'Europe's Non-ferrous Metals Producers Call for Emergency EU Action to Prevent Permanent Deindustrialisation from Spiralling Electricity and Gas Prices', Open Letter to the European Commission, 7 September 2022, https://eurometaux.eu/media/qnhn5k30/non-ferrous-metals-ceo-letter-on-energy-crisis-06-09-2022.pdf; and European Chemical Industry Council (Cefic), 'Energy Crisis: The EU Chemical Industry Is Reaching Breaking Point', position paper, October 2022, https://cefic.org/app/uploads/2022/10/Cefic_Position_energy_crisis.pdf.

5   See Peggy Hollinger et al., 'Will the Energy Crisis Crush European Industry?', *Financial Times*, 19 October 2022, https://www.ft.com/content/75ed449d-e9fd-41de-96bd-c92d316651da.

6   Andy Home, 'Power Problems Rein in Global Aluminium Output Growth', Reuters, 24 January 2023, https://www.reuters.com/markets/commodities/power-problems-rein-global-aluminium-output-growth-2023-01-23/; and 'Germany's Speira to End Rheinwerk Aluminium Smelting Due to Energy Costs', Reuters, 9 March 2023, https://www.reuters.com/markets/commodities/germanys-speira-end-rheinwerk-aluminium-smelting-due-energy-costs-2023-03-09/.

7   See EUROFER, 'European Steel in Figures 2023', https://www.eurofer.eu/assets/publications/brochures-booklets-and-factsheets/european-steel-in-figures-2023/FINAL_EUROFER_Steel-in-Figures_2023.pdf.

8   See Ludwig Burger, 'BASF Seeks "Permanent" Cost Cuts at European Operations', Reuters, 26 October 2022, https://www.reuters.com/markets/europe/basf-says-european-operations-need-be-cut-size-permanently-2022-10-26/; and Johanna Treeck, 'Mittel-kaput? German Industry Stares Into the Abyss', *Politico*, 10 November 2022, https://www.politico.eu/article/germany-industry-europe-energy-prices-basf/.

9   See Martin Arnold, 'German Energy Subsidy Savings Spark Battle Over How to Use Cash', *Financial Times*, 9 August 2023, https://www.ft.com/content/9432e1e9-8b19-465f-ab53-cbbe08b2b19a.

10 Even these figures do not tell the whole story: they represent an average cost of electricity from wind and solar facilities across whole countries, whereas the real competition is between traditional industrial hubs like the Ruhr and subnational locations elsewhere in the world where

renewable energy is especially cheap. The cost of electricity from the average large-scale solar facility built in 2021 was 65% higher than the cost of electricity from the most efficient solar farms. See International Renewable Energy Agency (IRENA), 'Renewable Power Generation Costs in 2021', Figure 3.7, p. 96, https://www.irena.org/publications/2022/Jul/Renewable-Power-Generation-Costs-in-2021.

[11] Based on data from *ibid.*, Figure 6.7, p. 151.

[12] The cost of onshore wind in Texas is $20–40 per megawatt hour compared to $58–76 in Europe. National Renewable Energy Laboratory, 'SLOPE: State and Local Planning for Energy', https://maps.nrel.gov/slope/. See also Mark Dyson, 'Wind and Solar Are Saving Texans $20 Million a Day', Rocky Mountain Institute, 3 August 2022, https://rmi.org/wind-and-solar-are-saving-texans-20-million-a-day/; and Wind Europe, 'Wind Energy Is the Cheapest Source of Electricity Generation', 29 March 2019, https://windeurope.org/policy/topics/economics/.

[13] See Alexandra Devlin et al., 'Global Green Hydrogen-based Steel Opportunities Surrounding High Quality Renewable Energy and Iron Ore Deposits', *Nature Communications*, vol. 14, article no. 2578, 4 May 2023, https://www.nature.com/articles/s41467-023-38123-2; Dolf Gielen et al., 'Renewables-based Decarbonization and Relocation of Iron and Steel Making: A Case Study', *Journal of Industrial Ecology*, vol. 24, no. 5, October 2020, pp. 1,113–25; and Hilton Trollip, Bryce McCall and Chris Bataille, 'How Green Primary Iron

Production in South Africa Could Help Global Decarbonization', *Climate Policy*, vol. 22, no. 2, January 2022, pp. 236–47.

[14] See Jonathan Packroff, 'Some Industries Might Have No Future in Germany, Economists Say', Euractiv, 2 August 2023, https://www.euractiv.com/section/economy-jobs/news/some-industries-might-have-no-future-in-germany-economists-say/.

[15] See Laura Pitel, Guy Chazan and Patricia Nilsson, 'Germany Plans to Subsidise Power-hungry Industries', *Financial Times*, 5 May 2023, https://www.ft.com/content/b4f6d51d-e023-4af0-bafc-b96650a0586d; and Hans von der Burchard, 'Germany Mulls New Energy Price Subsidy for Industries', *Politico*, 18 September 2023, https://www.politico.eu/article/germany-energy-price-subsidy-industry-competition/.

[16] See Riham Alkousaa, 'German Industry Leans on Berlin for Swift Carbon Storage Plan', Reuters, 23 August 2023, https://www.reuters.com/sustainability/german-industry-leans-berlin-swift-carbon-storage-plan-2023-08-23/.

[17] Secondary steel, which is mainly used in construction and is produced by processing scrap steel in an electric arc furnace, is not affected as significantly by differences in energy costs. The minimills that produce secondary steel often operate flexibly to avoid using electricity at peak times, making their energy costs more manageable. They also benefit from operating in proximity to steel scrap, which is abundant in highly populated, economically developed regions.

[18] See EUROFER, 'Map of EU Steel Production Sites', https://www.eurofer.eu/assets/Uploads/Slide1.PNG.

19   Based on investment costs for
     H2 Green Steel and HYBRIT in
     Sweden, and GravitHy in France. See
     Charles Daly, 'Mercedes-backed H2
     Green Steel Gets €4.55 Billion Debt
     Financing', Bloomberg, 24 October
     2022, https://www.bloomberg.
     com/news/articles/2022-10-24/
     mercedes-backed-h2-green-steel-gets-
     4-55-billion-debt-financing; Rachel
     Parkes, 'Green Steel Group Plans
     Giant Electrolyser Array in France for
     Hydrogen-derived "Direct Reduced
     Iron"', *Recharge News*, 30 June 2022,
     https://www.rechargenews.com/
     energy-transition/green-steel-group-
     plans-giant-electrolyser-array-in-
     france-for-hydrogen-derived-direct-
     reduced-iron/2-1-1249168; 'Sweden's
     H2 Green Steel Plans to Raise $1.65 bln
     for Boden Plant', Reuters, 24 April 2023,
     https://www.reuters.com/markets/
     commodities/swedens-h2-green-steel-
     plans-165-bln-fundraising-ft-2023-04-24/;
     and Veolia, 'Five Billion Euros to
     Produce Steel Using "Green Hydrogen"
     in Sweden', 22 December 2020, https://
     web.archive.org/web/20210307000740/
     https://www.planet.veolia.com/en/
     five-billion-euros-produce-steel-using-
     green-hydrogen-sweden.
20   See Alexandra Devlin and Aidong
     Yang, 'Regional Supply Chains for
     Decarbonising Steel: Energy Efficiency
     and Green Premium Mitigation',
     Energy Conversion and Management,
     vol. 254, February 2022.
21   See Thomas Koch Blank, 'The
     Disruptive Potential of Green Steel',
     Rocky Mountain Institute, September
     2019, p. 5, https://rmi.org/wp-content/
     uploads/2019/09/green-steel-insight-
     brief.pdf.
22   See Devlin et al., 'Global Green
     Hydrogen-based Steel Opportunities
     Surrounding High Quality Renewable
     and Iron Ore Deposits'; Gielen et al.,
     'Renewables-based Decarbonization
     and Relocation of Iron and Steel
     Making'; and Trollip, McCall and
     Bataille, 'How Green Primary Iron
     Production in South Africa Could
     Help Global Decarbonization'.
23   Devlin et al., 'Global Green
     Hydrogen-based Steel Opportunities
     Surrounding High Quality Renewable
     Energy and Iron Ore Deposits'.
     Another study found that import-
     ing green crude steel from Morocco
     would be 14% cheaper than local
     production in Germany and 24%
     cheaper than local production in
     Finland. Of the European countries
     studied, only Spain is cost-competitive
     with Morocco. Japan faces similar
     problems, with primary-green-steel
     production there using iron ore and
     hydrogen imported from Australia
     projected to be some 32% more
     expensive than simply importing the
     green steel from Australia in 2050.
     See Gabriel Lopez et al., 'Towards
     Defossilised Steel: Supply Chain
     Options for a Green European Steel
     Industry', *Energy*, vol. 273, article no.
     12736, 15 June 2023, https://www.
     sciencedirect.com/science/article/pii/
     S0360544223006308?via%3Dihub.
     Likewise, green steel imported into
     Western Europe from Namibia is
     likely to be 15% cheaper than green
     steel produced in Europe. See African
     Climate Foundation and SYSTEMIQ,
     'Namibia's Green Hydrogen Strategy:
     Key Questions + Initial Answers',
     January 2022, https://gh2namibia.

com/gh2_file_uploads/2022/09/
Namibias-Green-Hydrogen-
Opportunity-key-questions-initial-
answers-Jan-2022-_-SYSTEMIQ.pdf.

24 Global ammonia production
    stands at around 185m metric
    tonnes per year, with prices rang-
    ing from around $425 to $525 per
    metric tonne, depending on geog-
    raphy. See International Energy
    Agency, 'Ammonia Technology
    Roadmap: Towards More Sustainable
    Nitrogen Fertiliser Production',
    October 2021, https://iea.blob.core.
    windows.net/assets/6ee41bb9-
    8e81-4b64-8701-2acc064ff6e4/
    AmmoniaTechnologyRoadmap.
    pdf; and S&P Global, 'Platts
    Ammonia Price Chart', accessed
    20 October 2023, https://www.
    spglobal.com/commodityinsights/
    en/market-insights/latest-news/
    energy-transition/051023-interactive-
    ammonia-price-chart-natural-gas-
    feedstock-europe-usgc-black-sea.

25 International Energy Agency,
    'Ammonia Technology Roadmap', p. 72.

26 Based on the most favourable green-
    hydrogen-technology option – that
    is, dedicated variable renewable
    energy plus geological hydrogen
    storage or pipeline H2 storage – with
    renewable-energy costs at $10 per
    megawatt hour in the most favour-
    able locations compared to $25 in the
    best locations in Europe. See Mission
    Possible Partnership, 'Making Net-zero
    Ammonia Possible: An Industry-
    backed, 1.5°C-aligned Transition
    Strategy', September 2022, pp. 44, 59,
    https://missionpossiblepartnership.org/
    wp-content/uploads/2022/09/Making-
    1.5-Aligned-Ammonia-possible.pdf.

27 Conservative shipping costs for ammo-
    nia are $60–80 per tonne, with more
    optimistic estimates as low as $40.
    See Ministry of Economy, Trade and
    Investment of Japan, 'Fuel Ammonia
    Supply Cost Analysis (Interim Report)',
    September 2022, https://www.meti.
    go.jp/shingikai/energy_environment/
    nenryo_anmonia/supply_chain_tf/
    pdf/20220928_e0.pdf; International
    Energy Agency, 'The Role of Low-
    carbon Fuels in the Clean Energy
    Transition of the Power Sector', October
    2021, p. 39, https://iea.blob.core.
    windows.net/assets/01ca16c8-e493-475c-
    81c4-04ac5d3b9882/Theroleoflow-carbo
    nfuelsinthecleanenergytransitionsofthep
    owersector.pdf; and Kawakami Yasuaki,
    Endo Seiya and Hirai Harumi, 'A
    Feasibility Study on the Supply Chain
    of CO2-free Ammonia with CCS and
    EOR', Institute of Energy Economics
    Japan, February 2019, https://eneken.
    ieej.or.jp/data/8371.pdf.

28 See Emergen Research, 'Chlor Alkali
    Industry Overview', May 2023,
    https://www.emergenresearch.com/
    industry-report/chlor-alkali-market.

29 European Salt Producers'
    Association, 'Salt Uses: Chemical
    Industry', https://eusalt.com/
    about-salt/salt-uses/industry/.

30 Eurochlor, 'Chlor-alkali Industry
    Review 2021–2022: Euro Chlor on Its
    Transition Pathway', August 2022,
    https://www.chlorineindustryreview.
    com/wp-content/uploads/2022/08/
    Industry-Review-2021-2022.pdf.

31 Eurochlor, 'The Electrolysis Process
    and the Real Costs of Production',
    July 2018, https://www.eurochlor.
    org/wp-content/uploads/2021/04/12-
    Electrolysis-production-costs.pdf/.

32 Rough calculation based on desalination of seawater at 50% efficiency, requiring 18 cubic metres of seawater per kilogram of hydrogen, containing 1.94% chlorine by mass.

33 Ewa Manthey, 'Aluminium Smelter Shutdowns Threaten Europe's Green Transition', ING, 14 March 2023, https://think.ing.com/articles/aluminium-smelter-shutdowns-threaten-europes-green-transition/.

34 Peter Hobson, 'Sky-high Energy Costs to Fan Fire Under Aluminium and Zinc Prices', Reuters, 12 August 2022, https://www.reuters.com/markets/commodities/sky-high-energy-costs-fan-fire-under-aluminium-zinc-prices-2022-08-12/.

35 See 'Germany's Speira to End Rheinwerk Aluminium Smelting Due to Energy Costs'; and Home, 'Power Problems Rein in Global Aluminium Output Growth'.

36 International Aluminium Institute, 'Primary Aluminium Production', https://international-aluminium.org/statistics/primary-aluminium-production/.

37 CRU Consulting, 'Opportunities for Aluminium in a Post-Covid Economy', report prepared for the International Aluminium Institute, 28 January 2022, https://international-aluminium.org/wp-content/uploads/2022/03/CRU-Opportunities-for-aluminium-in-a-post-Covid-economy-Report.pdf.

38 European Commission, 'Energy-efficient Cloud Computing Technologies and Policies for an Eco-friendly Cloud Market', May 2020 (updated November 2020), https://digital-strategy.ec.europa.eu/en/library/energy-efficient-cloud-computing-technologies-and-policies-eco-friendly-cloud-market.

39 Kara Fox, 'Ireland's Data Centers Are an Economic Lifeline. Environmentalists Say They're Wrecking the Planet', CNN, 23 January 2022, https://edition.cnn.com/2022/01/23/tech/ireland-data-centers-climate-intl-cmd/index.html.

40 See Tracy Brown Hamilton, 'In a Small Dutch Town, a Fight with Meta Over a Massive Data Center', *Washington Post*, 1 June 2022, https://www.washingtonpost.com/climate-environment/2022/05/28/meta-data-center-zeewolde-netherlands/; and Netherlands Central Bureau of Statistics, 'StatLine: Hernieuwbare elektriciteit; productie en vermogen', https://opendata.cbs.nl/statline/#/CBS/nl/dataset/82610NED/table?ts=1617545569760.

41 Rough conservative estimate based on a capacity factor of 28% for onshore wind in the Netherlands, per 'StatLine'.

42 See Pieter Haeck and Antonia Zimmermann, 'Europe's Hidden Energy Crisis: Data Centers', *Politico*, 3 October 2022, https://www.politico.eu/article/data-center-energy-water-intensive-tech/.

43 See Laura Roddy, 'Doubt Over Tech Giants' €2bn Data Investment', *The Times*, 21 August 2022, https://www.thetimes.co.uk/article/doubt-over-tech-giants-2bn-data-investment-kzgks50gw.

44 See Government of the Netherlands, 'Kabinet beperkt mogelijkheid tot vestiging hyperscale data-centra', press release, 10 May

2022, https://www.rijksoverheid. nl/actueel/nieuws/2022/06/10/ kabinet-beperkt-mogelijkheid-tot-vestiging-hyperscale-datacentra.

45 Energy accounts for around 30% of greenhouse farms' operating expenditure and 53% of indoor vertical farms' operating expenditure, but operating costs are only around 20% of the total costs of operation. See Djavid Amidi-Abraham, 'Understanding Capital Expenses for Vertical Farms and Greenhouses', *Agritecture*, 25 January 2021, https:// www.agritecture.com/blog/2021/1/25/ understanding-capital-expenses-for-vertical-farms-and-greenhouses; Dafni Despoina Avgoustaki and George Xydis, 'Indoor Vertical Farming in the Urban Nexus Context: Business Growth and Resource Savings', *Sustainability*, vol. 12, no. 5, March 2020, p. 1,976; Robin Brumfield, 'Dealing with Rising Energy Costs', *Greenhouse Product News*, March 2007, p. 24, https://gpnmag.com/wp-content/uploads/dealingwithrising. pdf; and Katarzyna Kowalczyk et al., 'Comparison of Selected Costs in Greenhouse Cucumber Production with LED and HPS Supplemental Assimilation Lighting', *Agronomy*, vol. 10, no. 9, September 2020, p. 1,342.

46 See Precedence Research, 'Aviation Fuel Market', June 2023, https://www. precedenceresearch.com/aviation-fuel-market#; and Skyquest, 'Global Aviation Fuel Market', April 2023, https://www.skyquestt.com/report/ aviation-fuel-market.

47 See Mission Possible Partnership, 'Making Net-zero Aviation Possible', July 2022, p. 39, https://

missionpossiblepartnership.org/ wp-content/uploads/2023/01/Making-Net-Zero-Aviation-possible.pdf.

48 See World Economic Forum and McKinsey & Company, 'Clean Skies for Tomorrow: Delivering on the Global Power-to-liquid Ambition', May 2022, p. 18, https://www3.weforum.org/docs/ WEF_Clean_Skies_for_Tomorrow_ Power_to_Liquid_Deep_Dive_2022.pdf.

49 See International Energy Agency, 'Direct Air Capture: A Key Technology for Net Zero', 2022, https://iea.blob. core.windows.net/assets/78633715-15c0-44e1-81df-41123c556d57/ DirectAirCapture_ Akeytechnologyfornetzero.pdf; Sabine Fuss et al., 'Negative Emissions – Part 2: Costs, Potentials and Side Effects', *Environmental Research Letters*, vol. 13, no. 6, May 2018, https://iopscience.iop. org/article/10.1088/1748-9326/aabf9f; Royal Society and Royal Academy of Engineering, 'Greenhouse Gas Removal', September 2018, https:// royalsociety.org/-/media/policy/ projects/greenhouse-gas-removal/ royal-society-greenhouse-gas-removal-report-2018.pdf; and Marwan Sendi et al., 'Geospatial Analysis of Regional Climate Impacts to Accelerate Cost-efficient Direct Air Capture Deployment', *One Earth*, vol. 5, no. 10, October 2022, pp. 1,153–64.

50 Sendi et al., 'Geospatial Analysis of Regional Climate Impacts to Accelerate Cost-efficient Direct Air Capture Deployment'.

51 See Richard Haass, 'Deglobalization and Its Discontents', *Project Syndicate*, 12 May 2020, https://www. project-syndicate.org/commentary/ deglobalizaton-discontents-by-

richard-n-haass-2020-05; Mohamed El-Erian, 'From Near-shoring to Friend-shoring: The Changing Face of Globalisation', *Guardian*, 9 March 2023, https://www.theguardian.com/business/2023/mar/09/from-near-shoring-to-friend-shoring-the-changing-face-of-globalisation; Paul Krugman, 'The World Is Getting Less Flat', *New York Times*, 6 September 2022, https://www.nytimes.com/2022/09/06/opinion/the-world-is-getting-less-flat.html; Adam Posen, 'The End of Globalization?', *Foreign Affairs*, 17 March 2022, https://www.foreignaffairs.com/articles/world/2022-03-17/end-globalization; and Joseph Stiglitz, 'Getting Deglobalization Right', *Project Syndicate*, 31 May 2022, https://www.project-syndicate.org/commentary/deglobalization-and-its-discontents-by-joseph-e-stiglitz-2022-05.

52 The listed Western European states each have more than 200 people per square kilometre, compared with fewer than 25 in the listed Scandinavian states. See United Nations Department of Economic and Social Affairs, 'World Population Prospects 2022', 2022, https://population.un.org/wpp/.

53 Europe may produce fewer commodity chemicals (including ammonia, urea, nitric acid, chlorine, hydrochloric acid and caustic soda) and import them instead for use in the production of agrichemicals and consumer chemical goods, among other things. Some energy-intensive activity, such as primary-steel production, will continue in Europe, albeit at reduced levels. See, for example, Chris Bataille, Seton Stiebert and Francis G.N. Li, 'Global Facility Level Net-zero Steel Pathways; Technical Report on the First Scenarios of the Net-zero Steel Project', Net Zero Steel, 11 October 2021, http://netzerosteel.org/wp-content/uploads/pdf/net_zero_steel_report.pdf.

54 See European Union, 'Annual Detailed Enterprise Statistics for Industry', 2023, https://data.europa.eu/data/datasets/hvepsboxidbfx9oxmopg?locale=en; and Reiner Salzer et al., 'Employment and Careers of European Chemists (ESEC2)', *Chemistry: A European Journal*, vol. 24, no. 66, November 2018, pp. 17,370–88.

55 See International Aluminium Institute, 'Employment in the Global Aluminium Industry, 2019', May 2021, pp. 6–7, https://international-aluminium.org/wp-content/uploads/2021/06/Employment-in-Aluminium-Industry-Report-2021.pdf.

56 See 'Annual Detailed Enterprise Statistics for Industry'.

57 See European Commission, 'Steel: Preserving Sustainable Jobs and Growth in Europe', 16 March 2016, https://ec.europa.eu/commission/presscorner/detail/fr/MEMO_16_805.

58 See Alan Beattie, 'Brussels Defies US Pressure to Join Its Anti-China Gang', *Financial Times*, 23 October 2023, https://www.ft.com/content/a1b7aba6-9178-4e2f-809f-0e92aa261b54.

59 See Kadee Russ and Lydia Cox, 'Will Steel Tariffs Put U.S. Jobs at Risk?', Econofact, 26 February 2018, https://econofact.org/will-steel-tariffs-put-u-s-jobs-at-risk.

60 See, for example, Dalia Marin, 'The China Shock: Why Germany Is

Different', VoxEU, CEPR, 7 September 2017, https://cepr.org/voxeu/columns/china-shock-why-germany-different; and Robert Marschinski and David Martinez Turagano, 'Reassessing the Decline of EU Manufacturing: A Global Value Chain Analysis', European Commission, Joint Research Centre Technical Report, 2019, https://op.europa.eu/en/publication-detail/-/publication/5f21b462-1a33-11ea-8c1f-01aa75ed71a1#.

[61] See US Department of Defense, 'Assessing and Strengthening the Manufacturing and Defense Industrial Base and Supply Chain Resiliency of the United States: Report to President Donald J. Trump by the Interagency Task Force in Fulfillment of Executive Order 13806', September 2018, https://media.defense.gov/2018/Oct/05/2002048904/-1/-1/1/assessing-and-strengthening-the-manufacturing-and-defense-industrial-base-and-supply-chain-resiliency.pdf.

[62] See Christian Reichl and Michael Schatz, 'World Mining Data 2023', Federal Ministry of Finance, Republic of Austria, 25 April 2023, p. 155, https://world-mining-data.info/wmd/downloads/PDF/WMD2023.pdf; and US Department of the Interior, 'Mineral Commodity Summaries 2023', US Geological Survey, January 2023, p. 99, https://pubs.usgs.gov/periodicals/mcs2023/mcs2023.pdf.

[63] Reichl and Schatz, 'World Mining Data 2023', p. 161; and US Department of the Interior, 'Mineral Commodity Summaries 2023', p. 41.

[64] See Guillaume Gaulier and Soledad Zignago, 'BACI: International Trade Database at the Product-level. The

1994–2007 Version', CEPII Working Paper, 2010–23, http://www.cepii.fr/CEPII/en/bdd_modele/bdd_modele_item.asp?id=37.

[65] Such metals include chromium, manganese, molybdenum, nickel, niobium, titanium, tungsten and vanadium.

[66] See, for example, William D. Judge, Jaesuk Paeng and Gisele Azimi, 'Electrorefining for Direct Decarburization of Molten Iron', *Nature Materials*, no. 21, September 2021, pp. 1,130–6; and ArcelorMittal, 'Effectively Recycling Advanced Steels', https://automotive.arcelormittal.com/sustainability/recycling.

[67] See, for instance, Simon Nicholas and Soroush Basirat, 'New from Old: The Global Potential for More Scrap Steel Recycling', Institute for Energy Economics and Financial Analysis, December 2021, https://ieefa.org/wp-content/uploads/2021/12/The-Global-Potential-for-More-Scrap-Steel-Recycling_December-2021_2.pdf.

[68] See Sally Turner, '"Right Shoring" API Production in Europe', *Pharmaceutical Technology*, 22 March 2023, https://www.pharmaceutical-technology.com/features/right-shoring-api-production-in-europe-2/.

[69] See Devlin and Yang, 'Regional Supply Chains for Decarbonising Steel', Supplementary Data; and Devlin et al., 'Global Green Hydrogen-based Steel Opportunities Surrounding High Quality Renewable Energy and Iron Ore Deposits'.

[70] See 'Germany to Earmark 4 bln Euros Annually for Power Subsidy – Economy Minister', Reuters, 22 May

2023, https://www.reuters.com/world/europe/germany-earmark-4-bln-euros-annually-power-subsidy-economy-minister-2023-05-22/.

71 See European Commission, 'State Aid: Commission Approves German €550 Million Direct Grant and Conditional Payment Mechanism of up to €1.45 Billion to Support ThyssenKrupp Steel Europe in Decarbonising Its Steel Production and Accelerating Renewable Hydrogen Uptake', press release, 20 July 2023, https://ec.europa.eu/commission/presscorner/detail/en/IP_23_3928.

72 Based on 50–70 kg of hydrogen per tonne of steel, annual steel output of 26m tonnes, hydrogen shipping costs of $2 per kg in 2030 and $1 by 2050, and steel shipping costs of $50 per tonne. See 'Hydrogen Economy Outlook: Key Messages', BloombergNEF, 30 March 2020, https://data.bloomberglp.

com/professional/sites/24/BNEF-Hydrogen-Economy-Outlook-Key-Messages-30-Mar-2020.pdf.

73 See European Commission, 'Competition: State Aid Brief', issue 1/2023, July 2023, https://competition-policy.ec.europa.eu/system/files/2023-07/state_aid_brief_1_2023_kdam23001enn_TCTF_survey_0.pdf.

74 See World Energy Council, 'Policies for the Future: 2011 Assessment of Country Energy and Climate Policies', 2011, https://www.worldenergy.org/assets/downloads/PUB_wec_2011_assessment_of_energy_and_climate_policies_2011_WEC.pdf. The council noted the substance of the energy trilemma in 2010. See World Energy Council, 'Pursuing Sustainability: 2010 Assessment of Country Energy and Climate Policy', 2010, https://www.worldenergy.org/assets/downloads/PUB_wec_2010_assessment_of_energy_and_climate_policies_2010_WEC.pdf.

The United States, China and the Dispersal of Power

Baocheng Liu and Hilton L. Root

The rivalry between the United States and China will have unforeseen consequences for global stability, prosperity and governance that differ from those of the Cold War. The peculiarities of the countries' relationship and the differences in the global context make for a unique situation involving new risks. The interconnectedness of their economies and their mutual dependence on shared global systems impose a layer of complexity not found in the US–Soviet dynamic during the Cold War.

Similarities do exist. Fearful of a global realignment that is more favourable to its rival, each of the two nations is undertaking an intensifying diplomatic offensive. However, as the world economy fragments, power too will dissipate. Peripheral players will have greater freedom to improve their positions, and both superpowers will find that their diplomatic outreach costs more and achieves less. Understanding the changing structures of global networks, in which the ability of any single actor to influence linkages within the system has been greatly reduced, is vital to understanding the limitations of any grand strategy employed.

An analogy with Greek mythology is useful here. When the gods quarrelled, they frequently intervened in mortal affairs, manipulating events and influencing human lives. This interference limited the freedom of mortals to

Baocheng Liu is founder and director of the Center for International Business Ethics, as well as the Center for Green Entrepreneurship. **Hilton L. Root** is a professor of public policy at Schar School of Policy and Government at George Mason University and a visiting adjunct professor at the University of International Business and Economics in Beijing.

Survival | vol. 66 no. 1 | February–March 2024 | pp. 125–138   https://doi.org/10.1080/00396338.2024.2309079

shape their own destinies. For example, the dispute among the goddesses Aphrodite, Hera and Athena played a significant role in the outcome of the Trojan War. When they were at odds, gods often took sides and bestowed their protection on certain individuals or groups. Those denied this advantage faced greater challenges and limitations, and fear of divine retribution could restrict the freedom of mortals. But despite the gods' influence, Greek mythology emphasised the agency and choices of mortals, who were compelled to navigate a complex world in which they had to consider both the influence of the gods and their own desires and ambitions. Mortals still had the freedom to make decisions and pursue their own goals, and they could seek to play one god against another. Certain realms were presumptively exclusive to particular deities, and intervention in these domains by other gods could produce especially harsh reactions. The key lesson for the United States and China is that although the gods were immortal, they could severely harm one another.

Today, the processes of globalisation intertwine the actions and destinies of China and the US, revealing both their limitations and their intricate relational networks. Although the global power balance is proving to be more fluid and less predictable than either nation expected, the Chinese assessment of how mutual dependencies created by globalisation would imply changes in the political, economic and technological domains have proven more accurate than the assumptions of US policymakers.

American miscalculations

US policymakers made two erroneous assumptions about interconnectedness and mutual dependence. The first was that the US could 'own' globalisation and control how it would unfold in non-Western domains. Secondly, policymakers believed that the laws of the market would prevail over thousands of years of autocracy. These misconceptions underpinned the conditions placed on China for its entry to the World Trade Organization (WTO). The West did not appreciate that, owing to its size and internal unity, China might be able to engineer the 'sinicisation' of globalisation.

Although China explicitly stated its intentions to access the global marketplace for purposes of 'self-strengthening' in the 1990s, Western intellectuals disregarded the assertion on the view that greater interconnectedness via free trade would irresistibly put China on the path towards liberal democracy. This outlook became a load-bearing foundation of US global-development policy. Yet it marked a stark reversal of the Western thinking on US–China relations that had prevailed throughout the 1950s and 1960s. Then, as now, China opposed the American emphasis on human rights and personal welfare. But scholars such as John King Fairbank and Jonathan Spence, as well as many policymakers, considered the idea that the Chinese population could be liberated from their beliefs, values and ingrained acceptance of authoritarian centralisation unrealistic.[1]

The reversal of China's economic policies during the 1980s nurtured expectations that it was on a path towards greater alignment with Western values. But the United States failed to recognise that the Chinese approach to globalisation tracked with a view popular during the late-Qing reforms in the nineteenth century known as *zhongti xiyong*, meaning 'Chinese learning for fundamentals and Western learning for practical applications', that advocated the introduction of advanced Western technology without changing the imperial system.[2] The official expression addressing foreign investment is *liyong waizi* – 'taking advantage of foreign investment' – which implies expediency rather than enduring commitment.[3] In retrospect, it seems clear that China never intended to completely open its market for equal access by foreign enterprises, let alone to foreign ideas about governance.

Harnessing globalisation's inexorable logic

China and the United States started out with very different notions of how to approach globalisation. For the US, it was a way to showcase the welfare gains from the ideals of individualism and natural rights. For China, it was a vindication of austerity, collective effort and a philosophy of self-limitation. China consistently underlined that its cultural differences would not allow it to align its institutions with those of the West, and never intended to allow the West full access to the Chinese market and society. While conceding its deficiencies in science and technology, China has been determined to keep the locks and keys in its own hands to prevent a repeat of the forced opening that started with the Opium Wars in the mid-1800s. This constraint is evident in the slogan of the Westernization Movement (1861–95) of 'learning foreign skills for self-renewal', repurposed in Mao Zedong's 'turning foreign things to China's service' in 1964, Deng Xiaoping's open-door policy in 1978, and now Chinese President Xi Jinping's China-centric notion of 'dual circulations' intended to separate the domestic economy from the export economy.[4]

Chinese participation in the global economy never meant the renunciation of state planning as the paradigm for economic modernisation. On the contrary, Chinese leaders continue to believe that top-down execution is essential for China to surpass the West in the growth and distribution of national wealth. To this end, the state retains ownership of all land, and leasing it for real estate and industrial development is the main revenue stream for local governments. China endorses hybrid ownership among market participants, a blend of state-owned enterprises (SOEs), foreign-invested enterprises and private enterprises.

To emphasise the socialist nature of the market economy, private firms are deemed people-operated enterprises (*minying qiye*) and SOEs people-owned enterprises (*quanmin suoyou qiye*). Special Economic Zones, High-tech Development Zones and Free-trade Zones are all mechanisms for ensuring that foreign investment creates a 'bird-cage economy' that can bring in advanced technology and generate foreign-exchange earnings while remaining in a state-controlled system.[5] Every year, China's top national-planning agency, the National Development and Reform Commission, publishes guidelines for foreign investment that specify the priorities for different sectors and regions. 'Effective state combined with efficient market' is the reigning catchphrase. This approach blends elements of state-led planning and control with market-oriented reforms. Its source can be traced back to the economic reforms initiated by Deng in the late 1970s and early 1980s, and is deeply rooted in China's unique political and ideological framework. The domains in which state and market can find their respective competitive advantages is left to the state's freewheeling interpretation.

Sinicisation of globalisation

After the fall of the Berlin Wall, Western policymakers apprehended globalisation and capitalism as parallel, interconnected processes and assumed that a more open China would acquiesce to a more privately invested, market-oriented, liberal Western standard. In theory, this would render the centrally planned Chinese model unsustainable, and the resulting adaptations would transform

China's authoritarian political regime. The US expected to be the mentor and China to be the pupil, but it was caught flat-footed when US and European manufacturing jobs vanished as China's GDP and manufacturing exports surged.[6] Western policymakers simply hadn't anticipated how effectively China would manage the prevailing trends of competitive globalisation.

The demise of the Soviet Union as a self-reliant fortress demonstrated to China that rejecting global trade was a losing strategy. But in the Chinese political vocabulary, 'westernisation' connotes alienation, and China has never accepted the idea of global social and political norms. China also attributes the fall of the Soviet Union and other autocratic governments in part to the United States' instigation of colour revolutions and views the West's control of global media as an instrument for destabilising Chinese Communist Party (CCP) rule. At a critical inflection point in geopolitics, China decided to avoid the fate of the Soviet Union by fully participating in global value chains, but only in measured steps rather than by following prescriptions for rapid privatisation and dramatic liberalisation. Chinese economic reforms were precisely calibrated to avert ideological contamination by the West, which it viewed and continues to view as the primary threat to its national security. In fact, Chinese spokespersons have often promoted the view, diametric to the prevailing Western outlook, that globalisation will intensify divergent world views.

When Jiang Zemin, handpicked by Deng to head the CCP, made clear his commitment to join the world economy in March 1998, he also stated that China approached globalisation as an inexorable force whose stages, pathways and consequences could not be anticipated, and whose management must be determined by national interest: 'Economic globalisation is an objective trend of world economic development, from which none can escape and in which everyone has to participate.'[7] This sentiment was widely shared in a country that had experienced a century of violent change bringing foreign merchants, diplomats and eventually armies to its shores. Jiang consistently described globalisation as 'an objective tendency independent of man's will' and as a fierce race in which building comprehensive national strength was the goal. China, he said, was determined not to allow economic globalisation to become a conduit for the proliferation of Western values and further tip the balance of power in the West's favour.[8]

China's 2001 accession to the WTO thus required deft political manoeu-vring by Chinese reformers, led by Jiang. In 1997, he clarified the economic role of the state and the long-term goals of SOE reform during the 15th Party Congress, noting that, as paraphrased by Paul Heytens,

> the introduction of market mechanisms (stock markets and institutions of corporate governance such as shareholders' meetings) were consistent with a socialist market economy, and the state did not have to dominate every sector or have majority ownership in every enterprise in order to maintain broad control of the economy.[9]

These changes were essential to align China with international business norms, as stipulated in the agreement, and had to be accomplished within a one-year time frame. To win over the hardliners, Jiang bargained with the WTO for concessions and transitional periods that included provi-sions related to tariffs, non-tariff measures and intellectual-property rights. These provisions were designed to gradually bring China's trade and economic policies in line with WTO standards. Central planning did not disappear after China joined the WTO, but was redirected to setting out pragmatic blueprints for domestic growth and preparing the population for the impending globalisation shocks. Jiang insisted that these were not harbingers of democratic-governance reforms. China was willing to accept the scientific and technological imperatives of globalisation, as well the inevitability of universal consumerism, but not the prophecy of democratic and social convergence. He repeatedly stated his belief that no one country could drive the outcome of the economic forces at work, but that an open and integrated China would constrain US hegemony and have a powerful voice in global rule-setting.[10]

He had his reasons. Since the 1970s, a variety of factors have prompted the massive relocation of production from the developed world to emerging economies that are open to globalisation. They include environmental and labour movements, market saturation in high-income countries, and reductions in transportation and communication costs. Abundant low-cost labour, lax environmental standards and weak unions in emerging economies have also played a role. Firms recognised that they could compartmentalise production processes and relocate them to the most cost-competitive areas. Those who mastered the required transitions could build or join global value chains, leveraging extensive resources and financing to enhance their competitive edge. Consequently, trade flows and global payment patterns have produced changes in the product life cycle.[11]

The global integration of China's economy followed a different logic than that of Japan's or Korea's in the 1960s and 1970s. Their industrial restructuring meant establishing entire indigenous industries such as steel production and shipbuilding. The architects of Chinese market reforms saw that the key players at the emerging stage of globalisation were the multinational corporations (MNCs) that needed and oversaw vast commodity chains or production networks. Chinese policymakers viewed China's own economic challenges within the larger context of global industrial restructuring and focused on integrating their economy into transnational production and financial structures. Thus, they permitted foreign companies to link their entire global production lines to China as a part of their international sales networks. A key part of the strategy was to draw MNCs into joint ventures with Chinese partners as a means of gaining a shortcut to capital, technology, management skills and export channels. 'Technology for market access' was China's implicit quid pro quo. Most MNCs were happy to swap what they considered soft assets for equity positions in joint ventures or bundle their manufacturing knowledge with equipment in packaged transactions. But the MNCs' amenability enabled Chinese companies to quickly reach competitive levels of advanced technology and brand recognition. Furthermore, local employees who had come to understand the technologies and market channels started their own enterprises, cooperating or competing with their previous MNC employers.

Reconciling Chinese ethical relativism with Western universalism

The rise of China was based on its ability to absorb Western technology without absorbing Western idealism, individualism, market liberalism or democracy. Globalisation presents nations with four basic paths: absorption, accommodation, marginalisation or alienation.

Absorption implies a full embrace of globalisation and deep integration into the global economic, political and cultural systems. This would mean adopting international norms, practices and policies, potentially at the expense of some traditional or local practices. In economic terms, it could mean fully opening up to international trade and investment, leading to a more interconnected and interdependent relationship with the global economy.

Accommodation is a more selective approach to globalisation whereby a country adopts aspects of globalisation that align with its interests and values, while maintaining more control over certain sectors or cultural aspects. This path would involve a balancing act, with the country actively participating in global trade and investment, but on its own terms. For China, this could mean engaging in global trade and cooperation but also protecting certain strategic industries or maintaining controls over capital flows and information.

Marginalisation is a risk faced by countries that fail to effectively engage with the global system. For China, this risk could arise from global shifts in trade, such as moves towards regional trade agreements from which it is excluded, or from an inability to move up the value chain in global production. This path could lead to reduced international influence, limited access to global markets, and a potential loss of economic and technological progress.

Alienation refers to a country's path of active resistance or rejection of aspects of globalisation, perhaps due to perceived threats to its political system, culture or sovereignty. This might involve retreating from international agreements, reducing participation in global markets or promoting alternative systems and alliances. It could also produce policies that limit foreign investment, restrict the flow of information or prioritise domestic considerations over international ones in policymaking. This path could lead to increased tensions with other countries and result in a more isolated and self-reliant China.

So far, China has been willing to avoid either marginalisation or alienation. Xi's belief, however, is that China has travelled far enough in the direction of accommodation and paid its admission price. Having made many concessions to global norms, China will not succumb to absorption.

Xi's aim to promote Chinese civilisation is also driven by a desire to protect China from what his tutor on Western civilisation, Wang Huning, considers to be the West's Achilles heel: the sanctity of individual rights. This, Wang believes, will make it impossible for the US to create and sustain a value-unified nation, and speed political discord and the paralysing loss of a moral core that will spell Western decline. China too, he warns, is at risk of moral crisis caused by the dramatic impact of the country's environmental, technological and material advances.[12] Thus, at the 2016 celebration of the CCP's 95th anniversary, Xi asserted a doctrine of 'four confidences' in China's path, theory, system and culture. He unambiguously advocated exploiting market economics to bolster socialism under single-party leadership while following the four principles of China's constitution of 1982: socialist road, proletarian dictatorship, CCP leadership, and Marxist–Leninist and Maoist thought. In subsequent issuances of doctrine, Xi has repeated the view that cultural values that are not shared with the West underlie China's rise.

As an alternative to the 'end of history' narrative, which asserts that Western technology and science are embedded in Western values and social norms, Xi emphasises a 'community of shared future for mankind'. This concept, rooted in the Confucian notion that 'all under heaven is one family', is a world view under which each civilisation has its own unique contribution to make to the future of humanity. As such, economic globalisation should be inclusive, fostering a balanced relationship between East and West.[13] Conversely, though, economic globalisation will not be allowed to unshackle the Chinese population from its 3,000-year political traditions. As John Fairbank observed in 1966, some form of centralised Chinese authoritarianism is 'going to be with us for the foreseeable future and we are going to have to live with it'.[14]

Freedom of action in a fragmented world

China's self-strengthening has created a more complex international environment with multifaceted conflict dynamics. The most important of these are the ongoing tensions between China and the US, which have created opportunities for peripheral countries and secondary powers to redefine their strategic interests and alignments, recalibrate their foreign relations and exploit economic openings. They may foster stronger ties with their neighbours and other regional powers to collectively manage the repercussions of great-power competition. Smaller states might forge collective-security arrangements or regional dialogues to address shared security concerns stemming from the US–China conflict. A good example is how Southeast Asia – the region most vulnerable to superpower rivalry – is strengthening its existing multinational institutions and creating new ones, from the Association of Southeast Asian Nations to the Regional Comprehensive Economic Partnership and the Comprehensive and Progressive Agreement for Trans-Pacific Partnership.

Rather than cleave sharply towards one superpower or another, some states may choose not to align completely with either while maintaining relationships with both, maximising benefits and avoiding dependency. Smaller countries might strengthen their military capabilities or form new alliances and partnerships to balance against China. Secondary powers could explore alternative supply chains and trade partnerships, or strengthen existing ties with regional powers such as India, Russia or the European Union. Some small countries can leverage their strategic locations, resources or market access to extract trade concessions or foreign aid from both China and the US. For instance, US 'friend-shoring' – moving supply chains to aligned nations – would give developing countries opportunities they would not enjoy if the US continued to depend mostly on China for manufactured goods.

The wrinkle is that countries like Vietnam and India have national interests that do not always align with those of the US. Peripheral powers will not necessarily stay on the United States' side even if they are convinced that it will persist as the dominant power. The structure of the global political economy is becoming more densely connected, giving both the East and the West less leverage to exercise top-down control. Preventing China's rise will not perforce preserve the US-led international system, nor will Beijing's short-term goal of weakening the US automatically provide it with alternative bilateral ties. The world is pulling apart; it is not defecting to Beijing. Countries worry less about China overtaking the US and more about becoming autonomous strategic actors themselves so as to challenge the putative but weakened great powers. And as more countries gain strategic parity, each will have a greater incentive to seek the best outcome for itself, even at the expense of others and of system stability.[15] Athens and Sparta believed that the demise of one would be the triumph of the other. Instead, conflict made both weaker, and ultimately led to their decline. The tears of Athens were not the joys of Sparta.

* * *

During the Cold War, the US and the Soviet Union operated largely within different economic spheres, with minimal economic interaction and dependency. The Soviet Union was largely excluded from Western-led institutions. China and the United States are parts of a deeply integrated global financial system, with cross-border supply chains, investments, holdings and financial products. China is now a key member of international institutions such as the WTO, the International Monetary Fund and the World Bank. The United States relies on Chinese manufacturing for various goods, while China holds a substantial amount of US debt. Decoupling could trigger financial instability, affect currency values and have cascading effects on global financial markets, potentially leading to a global crisis. Even prolonged trade tensions could produce disruptions in supply chains, higher costs for consumers and producers, and reduced economic growth in China, the US and elsewhere. US–China friction can also obstruct international cooperation on global issues like climate change, public health and poverty reduction.

In Greek mythology, fate bound the gods in a mutual understanding of the limitations of their powers. Mortals too understood the boundaries of divine influence and manipulation. The binding and pervasive nature of globalisation will have an analogously complicated influence on the world's political economy, as well as the relationship between China and the United States.

Notes

[1] See, for example, John King Fairbank, *The United States and China* (Cambridge, MA: Harvard University Press, 1948); and Jonathan D. Spence, *To Change China: Western Advisers in* *China 1620–1960* (New York: Little, Brown and Co., 1969).

[2] See Junyu Shao, *Chinese Learning for Fundamental Structure, Western Learning for Practical Use? The*

Development of Late Nineteenth Century Chinese Steam Navy Revisited, PhD dissertation, King's College London, August 2015, https://kclpure.kcl.ac.uk/portal/files/46323975/2015_Shao_Junyu_11380711_ethesis.pdf.

3   See Sheng Zhang, 'Protection of Foreign Investment in China: The Foreign Investment Law and the Changing Landscape', *European Business Organisation Law Review*, vol. 23, no. 4, April 2022, pp. 1,049–76.

4   See Shin Oya, 'What China's "Dual Circulation" Strategy Means for the World', *Japan Times*, 3 November 2020, https://www.japantimes.co.jp/opinion/2020/11/03/commentary/world-commentary/china-dual-circulation-strategy/.

5   The reconciliation of socialist planning with market economics was elucidated as early as 1957, by Chinese economic planner Chen Yun by way of the concept of 'cage economics': the bird of the market is free to fly, but only within the cage of planning. See David M. Bachman, *Chen Yun and the Chinese Political System* (Berkeley, CA: University of California Press, 1985), p. 152.

6   See David H. Autor, David Dorn and Gordon H. Hanson, 'The China Shock: Learning from Labor Market Adjustment to Large Changes in Trade', National Bureau of Economic Research (NBER) Working Paper 21906, January 2016, https://www.nber.org/papers/w21906.

7   Quoted in Joseph Fewsmith, 'China and the WTO: The Politics Behind the Agreement', *NBR Analysis*, vol. 10, no. 5, 1 December 1999, https://www.nbr.org/publication/china-and-the-wto-the-politics-behind-the-agreement/.

8   See Thomas G. Moore, 'China and Globalization', *Asian Perspective*, vol. 23, no. 4, 1999, pp. 65–95.

9   Paul J. Heytens, '9 State Enterprise Reforms', in Wanda Tseng and Markus Rodlauer (eds), *China: Competing in the Global Economy* (Washington DC: International Monetary Fund, 2003), pp. 124–48.

10   See Permanent Mission of the People's Republic of China to the UN, 'Statement by H.E. Jiang Zemin, President of the People's Republic of China, at the Millenium Summit of the United Nations', 6 September 2000, http://un.china-mission.gov.cn/eng/zt/qiannianfenghui/200009/t20000906_8414140.htm.

11   The product-life-cycle theory developed by Raymond Vernon suggests that early in a product's life cycle all the parts and labour associated with that product come from the area where it was invented. After the product becomes adopted in world markets, production gradually moves away from the point of origin. In some situations, the product is imported by its original country of invention. See Charles W.L. Hill, *International Business: Competing in the Global Marketplace* (New York: McGraw Hill, 2011).

12   See, for example, N.S. Lyons, 'The Triumph and Terror of Wang Huning', *Palladium*, 11 October 2021, https://www.palladiummag.com/2021/10/11/the-triumph-and-terror-of-wang-huning/; and 'Wang Huning's Career Reveals Much About Political Change in China', *The Economist*, 12 February 2022, https://www.economist.com/china/2022/02/12/wang-hunings-career-reveals-much-about-political-change-in-china.

13 See Xi Jinping, 'Speech: Work Together to Build a Community of Shared Future for Mankind', Xinhua.net, 18 January 2017, http://www.xinhuanet.com/english/2017-01/19/c_135994707.htm.

14 John King Fairbank, 'Reflections on "The China Problem"', *Diplomat Magazine*, vol. 17, 1966, pp. 37–9.

15 On the network properties of power in international networks, see Hilton L. Root, *Network Origins of the Global Economy: East vs. West in a Complex Systems Perspective* (Cambridge: Cambridge University Press, 2020), pp. 227–52. In computing closeness (how tightly connected a node is to the network) and betweenness (the degree to which a node is a boundary-spanner) over time, both the US and China show signs of diminishing centrality, affording peripheral players more freedom.

Review Essay

The US Navy and the Western Pacific

James J. Wirtz

U.S. Naval Power in the 21st Century: A New Strategy for Facing the Chinese and Russian Threat
Brent Droste Sadler. Annapolis, MD: Naval Institute Press, 2023.
$39.95. 400 pp.

I once had the privilege of delivering a series of lectures on US national-security strategy to students at Kazakhstan's National Defense University. Armed with briefing slides culled from the latest government documents, I dutifully reported the Obama administration's thinking about security matters. I was greeted by a sophisticated audience, filled with officers who were well versed in military history, contemporary defence issues and the nuances of strategy articulated by the Prussian philosopher Carl von Clausewitz. Nevertheless, I was not prepared for their bemused and incredulous response to my pitch.

My briefing contained no mention of border defences, or new armoured vehicles, or the mobilisation of reservists to bolster deterrence. Instead, American strategy was all about global trade, global influence and globalisation. Fostering and protecting ocean commerce, international finance and worldwide communications – the flow of ideas, people, goods and money around the planet – was depicted as a source of US security and prosperity, and a matter of national destiny. American ideas and influence would shape

James J. Wirtz is a professor in the Department of National Security Affairs at the US Naval Postgraduate School. He recently updated Colin Gray's strategic history, *War, Peace and International Relations*, 3rd edition (Routledge, 2023).

 https://doi.org/10.1080/00396338.2024.2309081

political preferences, guiding the world towards Washington's rules-based order and a better way of life. The message delivered to that audience of continentally minded strategists was that American national security was based on a maritime strategy, one that reflected the ideas of Alfred Thayer Mahan, the intellectual father of the modern US Navy.

Limitations of naval statecraft

The Mahanian thinking that permeates US foreign and defence policy serves as the opening foil for Brent Droste Sadler's *U.S. Naval Power in the*

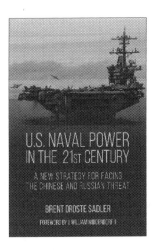

21st Century. It is apparently de rigueur for navalists to bemoan the fact that Washington has lost its maritime bearings, and Sadler adheres to this tradition by advocating the adoption of 'naval statecraft' – that is, the use of the US Navy 'to shape the environment in which security, diplomacy, and economics interact' – as an effective response to today's security challenges (p. 15). For Sadler, an American return to its Mahanian roots will help to produce the ships and capabilities needed by the US Navy to meet the challenge of today's great-power competition. Given America's bias towards a maritime strategy, using an updated version of Mahan's teachings to bolster popular support for a powerful navy will undoubtedly be well received by a receptive audience in the halls of Congress and on Main Street alike.

Although Sadler's concept of naval statecraft is somewhat narrow in scope – it highlights the economic stimulus and political goodwill that follow when US Navy warships make foreign-port calls or sign long-term ship-husbanding arrangements with local purveyors – the author offers a detailed description of the global maritime setting, and the technological and strategic challenges and opportunities facing navy officers today. Sadler dives into the nitty-gritty of port operations, telecommunications and logistical flows to demonstrate how these interact across the security, diplomatic and economic domains in a globalised world. He also highlights how the oceans shape military competition with Russia and China, and how this maritime setting is itself evolving – the melting Arctic ice cap might soon create a navigable Northwest Passage. Indeed, the strength of Sadler's effort lies in his description of the budgetary, administrative, technical and maintenance hurdles that are complicating efforts to keep the existing American fleet at sea and to rapidly expand the number of ships in the US Navy.

Sadler also identifies the techno-strategic challenges faced by the US Navy. The rise of great-power competition, especially the overwhelming Chinese maritime presence in the Western Pacific and the proliferation of advanced reconnaissance-strike complexes and long-range precision-strike capabilities, threatens the survivability of the carrier-centric US Navy. No longer can American forces be counted on to dominate vital waterways and leisurely conduct carrier raids against targets ashore. Instead, the navy finds itself outgunned and outranged by land-based systems in the Western Pacific, which is a rather circumspect way to describe the situation at sea. As one long-time denizen of the Pentagon put it: 'You can't lose the Fleet in defense of Taiwan, we need it to defend America.'[1] The days when the US Navy could sail up to virtually any littoral to reassure allies, intimidate potential opponents, interdict sea lines of communication or project power ashore are a thing of the past within the 'first island chain' encompassing the Kuril Islands, the Japanese archipelago, the Ryukyu Islands, Taiwan, the northern Philippines and Borneo.

Sadler identifies several developments that have led the navy to fall behind in its maritime competition with the People's Republic of China. For instance, efforts to secure a peace dividend following the end of the Cold War reduced shipbuilding, repair and maintenance facilities to such an extent that the size of the US fleet will shrink in the years ahead, regardless of the amount of money allocated to building new vessels. Decades will pass before the fleet can increase significantly because it will take that long to build the infrastructure required to increase the number of ships produced annually. Even if such facilities were available, the navy appears incapable of designing and building *useful* warships on budget and at scale: the *Zumwalt*-class destroyer and the Littoral Combat Ship designed in the 1990s turned out to be expensive failures, while the new *Ford*-class aircraft carrier has experienced endless cost overruns and delays in entering operational service. Sadler identifies a long list of new technologies – artificial intelligence, quantum computing, genetic engineering, nanotechnology – that could be incorporated into naval systems and weapons, but it is hard to imagine that the navy as an institution will quickly and successfully adapt to these breakthroughs when it cannot even build conventional warships. To his credit, Sadler mentions several nagging problems recently experienced by the navy that point to the existence of a corrosive organisational culture: corruption (the 'Fat Leonard' bribery scandal, in which officers from the US Seventh Fleet accepted bribes from a contractor in exchange for classified information); training and operational failures (ship collisions in 2017 and the 2020 USS *Bonhomme Richard* fire); and the navy's placement into receivership in 2020 when the Office of the Secretary of Defense reassessed its ongoing shipbuilding plans.[2] Nevertheless, Sadler is reluctant to draw the obvious conclusion from such failures that the US Navy is in an increasingly dire position in the Western Pacific. The problem is not a lack of congressional or public interest, or any deviation from Mahan's ideas, but rather the navy's own organisational failure.

Getting there from here

Because the techno-strategic challenge facing the US Navy is both extreme and imminent, simply doing more of the same is not a viable option for strengthening the US deterrent posture in the Western Pacific. For instance, Sadler's suggestion to engage in a naval arms race with China by building more multi-mission warships or even small nuclear-powered aircraft carriers that can be forward-deployed in contested areas is unrealistic, given the evident limitations of the maritime-industrial complex. Additionally, increasing the number of ships forward-deployed between the Asian littoral and the first island chain would only result in the loss of those units in the event of hostilities; they would be outnumbered and quickly overwhelmed by Chinese forces. The fate of the US Asiatic Fleet in the opening weeks of the Second World War offers a relevant historical precedent. Sadler suggests that reorganisation of the navy according to a new fleet structure might allow it to better adapt to various regional settings and foster the accumulation of local knowledge, and to distance itself from the existing joint command structure created by the 1986 Goldwater–Nichols Act. Yet such a move would not only draw the ire of Congress and the civilians within the US Department of Defense, but might also reduce the ability of the other services to support navy ships operating in the vicinity of the Asian mainland. By contrast, Sadler's call for increasing the size of the navy's autonomous fleet makes more sense, because autonomous vessels can be procured rapidly and relatively cheaply, adding significant near-term capability to a navy that is struggling to maintain its present size.

The recommendations offered in *U.S. Naval Power in the 21st Century* are grounded in the limitations of the navy's industrial base, personnel resources, budgetary realities and bureaucratic preferences, and the volume is filled with commonsensical and culturally acceptable recommendations that hold out some promise to prepare the US fleet for renewed great-power competition. More ships, more weapons and more sophisticated systems that enhance the way the navy operates, while not threatening existing career paths, traditional operations and other cultural preferences (such as a desire to increase the opportunities to command at sea), are reassuring and will be welcomed by most naval officers. Still, Sadler's work also suggests that the navy can't really get there from here – that more of the same will not create the military capability needed to defend Taiwan or to operate in the South China Sea in the event of hostilities. The navy lacks the infrastructure to build ships rapidly or even to maintain the ships it already has, while its recent efforts to design and build innovative warships are generally viewed as a failure. Navy strategists, designers and planners are encountering a growing number of new technologies that might form the basis of new systems or weapons, but knowledge of and experience with these technologies is limited. Standing midwatch on some bridge in the middle of the ocean is a poor place to acquire the education and experience needed to capitalise on emerging scientific and technological opportunities. Indeed, Sadler fails to mention the role education must play in preparing the naval workforce to use the new technologies that are entering the fleet at decreasing intervals, or that the navy as an institution is loath to replace a personnel system that is educating staff to meet past, not future, demands.

Sadler's book ultimately suggests that the only way the navy can get there from here is to undergo the kind of fundamental cultural, programmatic and operational change it experienced in summer 1942, when it decided to end its battleship programme following the completion of the four *Iowa*-class warships already under construction. Senior officers and civilians made the decision that the aircraft carrier would serve as the primary strike weapon of the surface navy, creating an approach to naval warfare that remains in place today. The navy now seems to have bet on autonomy as the dominant technical innovation of the coming decades, but we are still in the very early stages of this technological revolution and many details are far from being worked out. All the limitations faced by the navy today will complicate the introduction of autonomous systems into the fleet, and it remains unclear how the navy intends to fight with drones.

To accelerate the pace of this transition, the navy will have to not only redirect resources away from beloved weapons and systems, but also change itself in fundamental ways. This is the ultimate challenge facing Sadler's navy – it must quickly overcome its organisational culture and preferences to embrace new systems, weapons and ways of operation, a process that most of its officers will find profoundly unsettling. Nevertheless, the opponent in the Western Pacific is also working hard to facilitate the introduction of new and potentially transformational weapons, and to assess them in the only test that counts, in battle against the carrier-centric US Navy.

Notes

1 Bruce Stubbs, formerly of the US Navy Staff, Pentagon. Personal communication with author, March 2022.
2 See Paul McLeary, 'Congress Pumps the Brakes on Navy, Demands Answers from OSD', *Breaking Defense*, 20 July 2020, https://breakingdefense.com/2020/07/congress-pumps-the-brakes-on-navy-demands-answers-from-osd/.

Book Reviews

Politics and International Relations
Steven Simon

Hamas Contained: The Rise and Pacification of
Palestinian Resistance
Tareq Baconi. Stanford, CA: Stanford University Press, 2018.
$26.00. 368 pp.

This book is a bit long in the tooth for a review in 2024, but it qualifies because the present moment demands an understanding of Hamas as a social movement, political party and military force (or terrorist group, given that it pursues 'resistance' largely through acts of terrorism). Tareq Baconi's book meets this need and ought to be revised and updated in light of Hamas's attack on Israel on 7 October 2023 and its aftermath. Baconi relies primarily on a leading Hamas publication and on secondary literature for his source material, in contrast to other scholars who tend to use interviews with Hamas officials outside of Gaza, whether in Beirut, Doha or elsewhere, and within Gaza itself. These are shrewd interlocutors, however, and naturally tend to shape their remarks in ways that advance Hamas objectives rather than enrich analysis of the organisation. Depending – mostly – on the output of a single publication, as Baconi does, has its own limitations. When combined with close scrutiny of what Hamas actually does, however, it can be useful, especially when the author is as careful as Baconi is in this book. But, perhaps obviously, he cannot get inside the heads of the Hamas leadership.

The book's main virtue is its chronological format. It covers Hamas's relatively brief existence – compared, say, to the much longer lifespan of the Muslim Brotherhood from which it derived – year by year, thereby giving the reader a fairly clear sense of how Hamas's perceptions and strategies have changed over time, particularly after Israel's unilateral withdrawal from Gaza in 2005. Its main defect is that it does not mesh this evolutionary account with its Israeli cognate. Such a critique must be followed by an apology; this was not what Baconi aimed to do, and he can't be blamed for the absence of something he had not set out to cover. The literature on this topic and our overall understanding, however, would be greatly enriched by a book that meshed these parallel processes.

Several things stand out in Baconi's detailed account. The author painstakingly registers every instance in which Hamas has, in his view, signalled its willingness to depart from its charter and abide by whatever agreement the Palestine Liberation Organization (PLO) – the legal representative of the Palestinian people – reached with Israel. At the same time, Hamas has waged an unremitting campaign to supplant the Palestinian Authority, the entity created to govern the occupied territories, and which embodies the PLO within the territories – and, as it did so successfully in the mid-1990s, to destroy the Israeli–Palestinian peace process by hammering Israel with terrorist attacks. Thus, as true as it might be that Hamas will abide by whatever outcome the PLO accepts in the form of a final-status accord, the organisation is committed to replace the Palestinian leadership before it is in a position to reach such an agreement. The list of Hamas overtures and signals regarding a readiness to accommodate to Israel's existence was fascinating also because it underscored the importance of clarity in diplomacy and bargaining in general. Although ambiguity, as the saying goes, can be constructive where it creates space within which parties can probe, test and negotiate various formulas, in some contexts it can be worse than useless. And, as Baconi concedes, many of the Hamas initiatives he recounts were very subtle indeed and, amid a welter of conflicting signals, virtually inscrutable to Israelis. This is not to say that Baconi is incorrect in his assessment of these signals as genuine in some sense, only that the framing and delivery was too vague to make an impression.

The author is no Pollyanna, however. He lays out vividly the nihilistic world view that has complicated Hamas's interactions with Israel and by extension the Palestinian Authority. His analysis of the centrality of 'resistance' as an organising principle and *raison d'être* that paradoxically hobbled the organisation's ability to advance the goal of independence repays the effort of reading Baconi's book many times over. In addition, Baconi exactingly dissects two other phenomena central to the current crisis. The first is the bifurcation of Hamas's leadership into a kind of government in exile and another, whose members had spent decades in Israeli prisons, within Gaza itself. One can well see who had the upper hand. The second is the Hamas side of the gigue it danced with successive

Israeli governments to wrongfoot the Palestinian Authority and strengthen its own control over Gaza. Lastly, as the title suggests, the author shows that even deeply informed individuals had no idea what was to come on 7 October.

Meir Kahane: The Public Life and Political Thought of an American Jewish Radical
Shaul Magid. Princeton, NJ: Princeton University Press, 2021.
£30.00/£37.00. 296 pp.

The ongoing crisis in Gaza has raised the profile of a slower-moving, less intense crisis on the West Bank. Indeed, some commentators have argued that one of the many reasons Israel was vulnerable to attack by Hamas on 7 October was the redeployment of soldiers from the military's Southern Command, responsible for Gaza, to Central Command, which oversees security in the West Bank. The shift from one command to the other was necessitated by a surge of Israeli-settler attacks against Palestinian villages. The purpose of these raids was to push the Palestinian farmers off their land. There was the inevitable resistance, which took Israeli lives. The spiralling mayhem required additional troops to suppress. This situation has been nurtured by two members of the current Israeli government, Itamar Ben-Gvir and Bezalel Smotrich. Between them, with assistance from a third, smaller party, they won 600,000 votes in the November 2022 parliamentary election. This entitled them to powerful positions in the cabinet: Ben-Gvir as minister of national security and head of the Border Police, which has day-to-day responsibility for the West Bank (and Jerusalem); Smotrich as finance minister and deputy minister of defense for the West Bank. They are ethnonationalists, who advocate the expulsion of Arabs from the West Bank and, according to a recent remark by one of them, from Gaza.

Shaul Magid, a research fellow at Dartmouth College, has written a book that explains the ideology that drives Smotrich, Ben-Gvir and their cohort. This was not Magid's primary objective. His concern was to use the figure of his subject, Meir Kahane, as a 'lens' to explore tensions within American Judaism. But Kahane, who was assassinated in 1990, was also an important player in Israeli politics. He had been an Orthodox rabbi in New York before immigrating to Israel in 1971. In the overheated politics of the 1960s, as urban blacks repudiated their partnership with American Jews, Kahane created the Jewish Defense League (JDL), a militant organisation intended to protect Jewish communities adjacent to black neighbourhoods in the grittier areas of New York City. Given the iconography of militancy, limited as it is, the JDL logo looked startlingly like the logo emblazoned on Hizbullah's flag when that organisation emerged in the 1980s. Magid notes that Kahane's critique of liberal American Jews mirrored the thinking of radicalised blacks. Just as integration, on this view, demanded that blacks become white, so too, in Kahane's view, did the assimilation of Jews into American society require them to shed what made them Jews. Acceptance therefore meant annihilation, a bitter paradox.

Upon his move to Israel, he formed the Kach ('Thus') party, whose agenda was to demolish the conceit that in an Israeli context, there was no logical or feasible path toward a state that was both democratic and Jewish. His incendiary rhetoric on this point got him expelled from the Knesset in 1984. Although, as Magid observes, Kahane was subsequently airbrushed from Jewish history and the evolution of Zionism, he had a profound effect on the development of Israeli party politics. For the moment, his spiritual heirs have the whip hand.

Zionism: An Emotional State
Derek J. Penslar. New Brunswick, NJ: Rutgers University Press,
2023. $27.95. 284 pp.

Derek Penslar is a professor of Jewish Studies at Harvard University and, among other things, a historian of Zionism. As co-chair of Harvard's committee on campus anti-Semitism, he has come under fierce attack for saying that there is indeed a problem, but outsiders were making it appear worse than it is. In this book, he applies research in the area of emotion to an understanding of Zionism. That, at any rate, is the theoretical framework for an attempt to explain why the Zionist movement succeeded, why it is so reviled, and how Zionism itself came to revile – hate – its opponents. Much of this seems like common sense, although the theorisation of emotion in politics and international relations, as Penslar relates it, does shed interesting light on the phenomenon. Emotions, he says,

> have been linked with desire. Positive emotions respond to the fulfillment of desire or to the anticipation and expectation of its realization. In contrast, negative emotions are generated by the failure to obtain the object of desire or by the anticipation of that object's loss. Like positive emotions, negative ones vary greatly in intensity. (p. 213)

Alternatively, 'hatred is an alloy of negative emotions and, like an alloy, is more durable and enduring than its component parts' (p. 213). The author quotes an emotions scholar, who explains that 'while anger is focused on the actions of target objects and fear on the consequences of events, hatred is exclusively focused on the object itself' (p. 213). Penslar elaborates on this, observing that long-term grievances over perceived wrongdoings, resentments against perceived social inequities, and senses of constant threat feed a desire to separate oneself entirely from an Other, to remove that Other from one's midst, or even to annihilate the Other wherever it may be found. (p. 213)

'The hated object', he writes, 'is perceived as noxious, dangerous, or, in theological terms, evil' (p. 213). Penslar observes that 'as a cognitive routine, hate anchors an individual's sense of selfhood and attachment to a community' (p. 213). Startlingly, he describes the co-dependency of hater and the object of hate as 'bound together: the former depends on the latter just like a lover on the beloved' (p. 213). In terms of Israeli–Palestinian relations, this rings oddly true. The idea is certainly hard to argue with. For Penslar, understanding the gravitational appeal of Zionism for Jews, the animosity it arouses in non-Jews and the reciprocal hatred that anti-Zionists arouse in Zionists requires that we keep these concepts in mind.

Although this conceptualisation of emotions and their implications for Zionism and its opponents is surely useful, the value of the book lies more in Penslar's superb distillation of the intertwined histories of Zionism and anti-Zionism. The Gaza crisis has moved this history to centre stage; indeed, it is no longer history. It has become, inevitably, entangled with the questions, what is the difference between anti-Semitism and anti-Zionism, and how do we know when the one permeates the other? Penslar tackles these complicated questions with wisdom, sensitivity and style.

Islam, Authoritarianism, and Underdevelopment: A Global and Historical Comparison
Ahmet T. Kuru. Cambridge: Cambridge University Press, 2019.
£26.99. 316 pp.

Ahmet Kuru offers an exceptionally lucid approach to the seemingly perennial question regarding the parlous state of the modern Middle East: what went wrong? Bernard Lewis posed the question in just this way in his January 2002 piece in the *Atlantic* and answered it, in a word, with 'Islam'. As the crisis in Gaza unfolds, the question is perhaps even more urgent than it was in the wake of the al-Qaeda attacks of 11 September 2001, which prompted Lewis's influential article (and subsequent book). Kuru takes a more nuanced approach. His historically informed work on political economics follows in the footsteps of an earlier book by Timur Kuran, *The Long Divergence: How Islamic Law Held Back the Middle East* (Princeton University Press), reviewed in the June–July 2011 issue of *Survival*. Kuran argued that

Islamic law constrained the emergence of stock-traded companies in the Middle East just as these were becoming a feature of European economic activity. This in turn limited the growth of Muslim firms, reducing their relative competitiveness. Kuru's explanation hinges on class relations in the Muslim world during the medieval period, rather than the contemporary structure of business entities or, as Lewis contended, on the humiliation of the Muslim world following its eclipse by the West, and its inability to integrate European scientific and technological advances with Islamic culture. In this respect, Lewis was echoing the great Salafist reformers of the late nineteenth century. Kuru's objective is to explain the political economy of the Middle East without relying on the allegedly pernicious effect of Islamic doctrine, or the undeniable impact of European colonisation.

These competing views persist in part because there is much to be said for them, if not as much as can be said against them. There was an Islamic element among the many other contributing factors to today's Middle East malaise, and European colonial domination was violent, exploitative, degrading and, in the context of Middle Eastern societies, divisive. As Elizabeth Thompson showed in her landmark account of French political interference in mandatory Syria, *Colonial Citizens: Republican Rights, Paternal Privilege, and Gender in French Syria and Lebanon* (Columbia University Press), colonial powers have much to answer for. On the other hand, as Kuru demonstrates in detail, the political and economic deterioration within the Middle East was well under way before the advent of European colonialism. Prior to the 'crisis', in Kuru's phrase, of the twelfth to fourteenth centuries, the Islamic world was more advanced than Christian Europe in the sciences and philosophy. There can be little doubt that Islam was an important factor in the Mediterranean world and Middle East during that period.

Kuru takes the reader through the gap between essentialist readings of the Koran and anti-colonial philippics to an alternative explanation for current regional woes. He argues that in the eleventh century, the clerical establishment – the ulema – forged an alliance with Muslim militaries that served their mutual interest. The ulema gained access to state resources and control over education. This enabled the state to co-opt the ulema, thereby neutering a source of opposition to it. This ended a de facto separation of church and state that had been vital to development. The work of the ulema, as a result, was no longer privately funded and essentially independent. Free inquiry was crowded out by the new dispensation, just as church and state were beginning to separate in Christian Europe. This intriguing argument will certainly be contested in the future, but for the moment it will likely hold sway.

Indigenous Continent: The Epic Contest for North America
Pekka Hämäläinen. New York: Liveright, 2022. $40.00. 592 pp.

The Gaza war is shrouded in a war of epithets, as are all wars, going back, for example, to the Jewish war against the Romans in the first century CE, when the Jewish rebels were referred to exclusively as 'bandits'. In the current instance, the Palestinians, in their opponent's narrative, are terrorists, while Israel is branded as a settler-colonial state. The latter term was enshrined in the discourse of the left by Rashid Khalidi, a professor at Columbia, in his 2020 book *The Hundred Years' War on Palestine: A History of Settler Colonialism and Resistance, 1917–2017* (Metropolitan Books), a tour de force that merits a review of its own. The settler-colonial label, regardless of its analytical relevance, is now part of a powerful, mobilising rhetoric alongside the ubiquitous chant, 'from the river to the sea, Palestine will be free'. Pekka Hämäläinen's new book offers a perspective on the phenomenon by narrating an indisputable case of settler colonialism, while shedding light on a lesser-known but vital dimension of American history.

Hämäläinen, Rhodes Professor of American History at Oxford, made his mark with two previous books on the Comanche and Lakota, important indigenous peoples. The first was a thrilling portrayal of a mounted society, ruthless and powerful, that, in Hämäläinen's telling, established an empire rooted in the American southwest on the basis of a 'grass politics'. Immense grasslands enabled the Comanche to breed vast herds of horses; this made them highly mobile, like Mongols in a different setting, giving them huge reach. Combined with their cultivation of mounted-combat skills, this won them an empire, sustained by trade in horses in exchange for guns, food and other goods essential to their communities. This book established Hämäläinen as the *enfant terrible* of American studies because he focused on the indigenous population, previously understudied in the academic literature, but also because he depicted the Comanchería as an empire, which seemed to trivialise the imperial interventions of the Spanish, British and French, the true villains in the story.

In his latest work, he includes but also moves beyond the Comanche and Lakota to the Sioux and Ohio River Valley. In addition to covering more demographic and geographic ground, he covers a wider time frame, from the seventeenth century through to 1890. His corrective, if not quite revisionist, purpose is signified by the book's title, *Indigenous Continent*. His aim is to show that until the early nineteenth century, the phrase 'colonial America' misrepresents the reality of indigenous dominance on the continent. While the colonial population was confined to a narrow strip on the east coast, indigenous peoples controlled the 'vast interior' and its resources. The penetration of the hinterland by white peoples was either contested and reversed, or persisted at the pleasure of the indigenous population. Hämäläinen says, significantly, that

> time and again, and across centuries, Indians blocked and destroyed colonial projects, forcing Euro-Americans to accept Native ways, Native sovereignty, and Native dominance. This is what the historical record shows when American history is detached from mainstream historical narratives that privilege European ambitions, European perspectives, and European sources. (p. x)

Indeed, he claims, perhaps correctly, that there 'was a four-centuries-long war', in which 'Indians won as often as not' (pp. xii, xiii).

At the same time, the author paints a hideous picture of indigenous peoples' decline. Reconciling his broad claims about indigenous agency and effectuality with his parallel narrative of a population decimated by disease, outmatched militarily and swamped demographically – a process already under way with the great Puritan migration of the mid-1600s – demands a robust capacity to manage cognitive dissonance. Indeed, this raises the question of how there is still an indigenous population in the United States. There are a number of plausible explanations, but one in particular, advanced by other scholars, seems pertinent. From the Constitutional Convention onward (1787–89), the great tribal confederations deployed observers and lobbyists, as we would now call them, to represent their interests. In the nineteenth century, indigenous people relied on the courts to protect their equities and won important decisions. Their engagement over time with the United States judiciary, Congress and the executive branch could scarcely reverse a tragic fate or nullify the racist hostility of other Americans, but it did help them survive despite the odds.

Russia and Eurasia
Angela Stent

Getting Russia Right
Thomas Graham. Cambridge: Polity, 2023. £25.00. 272 pp.

There are two classic Russian questions about any problem: who is to blame, and what is to be done? In his trenchant critique of what went wrong in US–Russian relations after the Soviet collapse, Thomas Graham has answers for both. The United States, he writes, is to blame for the deterioration in ties prior to 2014, and thereafter Russia is to blame. After the Russia–Ukraine war ends, Washington needs to renegotiate relations with Moscow and respect its legitimate interests as a great power 'which entails, as all great-power relationships do, making trade-offs and compromises to manage the inevitable competition responsibly' (p. 5).

The US attempt to integrate post-Soviet Russia into Euro-Atlantic structures as a free-market democracy failed, Graham argues, because Washington did not understand Russian realities and needs, instead seeking to impose its own values and organisational structures on a society for which they were inappropriate. Graham is particularly critical of the Clinton administration's policies, which were imposed without offering the Yeltsin administration much input into the programmes.

Given Russia's historically expansionist tendency to absorb its neighbours to gain strategic depth, it was inevitable that under Boris Yeltsin and Vladimir Putin Russia would continue to believe that being a great power with a *droit de regard* in its neighbourhood was necessary for survival. Graham argues that the creation of a Euro-Atlantic security system without Russia and Washington's refusal to concede Moscow a sphere of influence in the post-Soviet space are the major reasons why relations deteriorated. Russian geography and history have 'conspired to embed a profound sense of vulnerability and insecurity in the Russian psyche' (p. 42).

US–Russian relations did show some promise in the aftermath of 9/11, but, says Graham, the Bush administration's refusal to treat Chechens in the same way as al-Qaeda terrorists, as well as its 'Freedom Agenda', support for colour revolutions and war in Iraq, soured Putin. And although the Obama administration paid less attention to Russia, its support of the United Nations resolution that led to Muammar Gadhafi's grisly demise enraged Putin further.

Graham has several suggestions for how to re-engage Russia after the war with Ukraine ends. The US and Russia must resume strategic-stability talks immediately. The US should rebuild a European security system that includes Russia, and should encourage greater European strategic autonomy. NATO should not admit any more members. Furthermore, Washington should work to persuade Moscow to distance itself from Beijing.

Perhaps most controversially, Graham argues that Washington and Moscow will have to negotiate an end to the war in Ukraine, because the Kremlin will only negotiate with the United States. Ukraine and Europe will not be in the room, although they will be consulted. He offers possible scenarios for what these negotiations would involve, but neutrality for Ukraine is a given. Needless to say, these proposals will generate robust discussion as the Russia–Ukraine war continues unabated and Putin looks to the March 2024 presidential election to vindicate his 'special military operation'.

Red Arctic: Russian Strategy Under Putin
Elizabeth Buchanan. Lanham, MD, and Washington DC:
Rowman & Littlefield and Brookings Institution Press, 2023.
£30.00/$37.00. 248 pp.

In 2007, Russian polar explorer and Duma member Artur Chilingarov, on an expedition to the North Pole, planted a Russian flag on the Arctic Ocean seabed. 'The Arctic is Russian', he announced to onlookers, explaining that 'the North Pole is an extension of the Russian coastal shelf' (p. 40). Since then, Russian designs on the Arctic have come under increasing scrutiny.

In her examination of Russia's Arctic strategy under Vladimir Putin, Elizabeth Buchanan refutes those who argue that the Arctic is becoming a new focus of great-power competition that will lead to a new cold war. On the contrary, she claims, the Arctic is one area where Russia pursues a cooperative agenda. This will continue, because it is in Moscow's interest to work with the West in this area. Indeed, Arctic cooperation could be the area in which Russia and the West resume their engagement once the Russia–Ukraine war is over.

In 1926, the USSR claimed the entire Arctic area adjoining the polar coast. Josef Stalin viewed the Arctic as a showcase for Soviet patriotism and the triumph of socialist industrialisation. After his death, interest in the Arctic waned until Mikhail Gorbachev, who focused on the Arctic as a zone of peaceful cooperation. Under Putin, interest and activity in the Arctic has greatly increased.

Buchanan argues that Russia is the largest Arctic stakeholder in terms of territory and is a legitimate player there. Its interests in the Arctic are both economic and military. The Arctic has the world's largest unexplored hydrocarbon reserves, which Russia seeks to exploit. Buchanan claims that Russia has not used energy as a strategic weapon in an Arctic context. Transportation is also a major Russian focus, since climate change has opened up the Northern Sea Route. Today, the Arctic accounts for 10% of Russian GDP and 20% of its exports, but that could significantly increase in the future. The key Russian decision-makers for the Arctic are Security Council head Nikolai Patrushev, Defence Minister Sergei Shoigu, Rosneft CEO Igor Sechin, Gazprom CEO Alexey Miller and oligarch Gennady Timchenko.

Red Arctic was completed before the 2022 Russian invasion of Ukraine, and in an afterword Buchanan argues that the war has not changed Russian behaviour in the Arctic. However, the Arctic Council, which has been a key venue for Russian cooperation with the West, has suspended Russian participation since the invasion. Russia held the presidency of the council from 2021–23 and has now handed it to Norway. Russian militarisation of the Arctic has increased, along with cyber and disinformation operations. And Russia is now cooperating with China, India and the United Arab Emirates in the Arctic.

Buchanan concludes by admitting that the 'age of Arctic exceptionalism is gone: the region is no longer a protected sphere of Russia–West engagement and dialogue' (p. 160). With greater Chinese activity in the region, plus new players that Russia is bringing in, the region will become more crowded, and new tensions could arise in the next decade.

The Russian Way of Deterrence: Strategic Culture, Coercion, and War
Dmitry (Dima) Adamsky. Stanford, CA: Stanford University Press, 2023. $26.00. 226 pp.

As the world watches with consternation how Russia is waging war against Ukraine, Dmitry Adamsky has published a timely and enlightening book on what he terms 'deterrence *à la Russe*'. He presents a rich analysis of Russian strategic culture focused on Russia's unique approach to coercion, which differs significantly from that of the West. This, he argues, is a product of Russia's history, culture and ideational influences.

Adamsky provides a detailed analysis of the evolution of Russian views in the post-Soviet era. Deterrence was not a central component of Soviet strategic thought and military art, but, after the Soviet collapse, 'this concept would become almost the Holy Grail of the Russian military brass … Deterrence *à la Russe* is a holistic construct, as it seeks to synthesize nuclear, conventional and non-kinetic forms of influence within one scheme of *strategic deterrence*' (pp. 23, 39, emphasis in original). He views 2014 – when Russia annexed Crimea and launched a war in the Donbas – as a watershed year in the evolution of Russian thought and action, the culmination of a series of events beginning with Vladimir Putin's 2007 speech at the Munich Security Conference, followed by the 2008 invasion of Georgia and the 2015 intervention in Syria.

The initial stage of the 2022 Russian invasion of Ukraine, in Adamsky's view, revealed traditional Russian pathologies: recklessness, negligence and carelessness. It also highlighted the gap between sophisticated military theory and the ability of the Russian state to implement it. The weakness of Russia's strategic–managerial culture also contributed to the failure of Russia's plan to take Kyiv in three days.

Nevertheless, while the West was unable to deter Russia from invading Ukraine, Russia was able to deter NATO from intervening in the war. This was largely because the United States was self-deterred by the understanding that a direct NATO–Russia confrontation could escalate into a nuclear war. Over the past two years, the Kremlin has periodically used the threat of tactical-nuclear-weapons use in Ukraine to deter the United States from providing weapons to Kyiv that could reach deep into Russian territory.

How do the Russians evaluate the effectiveness of deterrence *à la Russe*? After the Russia–Ukraine war began, one could argue that Russian coercive signalling achieved the opposite of what the Kremlin intended. The majority of Ukrainians will despise Russia for generations to come; Ukraine has moved closer to the European Union and NATO; and Finland has joined NATO and Sweden soon will, both countries having abandoned their traditional neutrality. NATO has beefed up its presence along Russia's borders, Europe has largely weaned itself from Russian hydrocarbons, and Russian informational operations have led to the establishment of new organisations in NATO and the United States to counter Russian cyber threats.

Adamsky concludes by asking whether the Russian military establishment is capable of self-criticism, and whether there will be a post-mortem after the war is over. We may have to wait some time for answers.

Soviet Self-hatred: The Secret Identities of Postsocialism in Contemporary Russia
Eliot Borenstein. Ithaca, NY: Cornell University Press, 2023.
$22.95. 204 pp.

Eliot Borenstein analyses how Russians have dealt with the trauma of the Soviet collapse and the quest to find new identities as they have built a new country over the past three decades. He examines fiction, films, jokes, songs and internet memes to paint a complex and often contradictory picture of how post-socialist Russians have coped with a loss of status and uncertainty about who they are.

He focuses on four different identities – all of which, as he points out, refer to men, not women – that have emerged since 1992. The first is the 'Sovok', 'the yokel who embodied stereotypes of Soviet backwardness', as famously caricatured by Sacha Baron Cohen in the film *Borat* (p. 146). The Sovok is a descendant of the 'Soviet man', described by the sociologist Yuri Levada as 'isolated', 'simplified', easily 'mobilized' and subject to 'doublethink' (p. 38). The Sovok has a limited understanding of things, and passively follows what the government tells him to do.

The second identity is the 'Vatnik', a belligerent patriot who accuses anyone who criticises any aspect of Russian life of 'Russophobia', a term increasingly used by the Kremlin. The Vatnik has become more prominent since the 2022 Russian invasion of Ukraine, and Ukrainians use the term to refer to the Russian enemy. Borenstein describes the Vatnik identity as being not only a representation of Putin-era aggressive patriotism but also a symbol of Russia's domestic polarisation.

A third identity is that of the 'New Russian', a term that first appeared in 1992. The New Russian is rich, gaudy and tasteless, and has accumulated assets in opaque ways. He is not necessarily an oligarch, who is richer and behaves in a more restrained way. New Russians can be successful or would-be business-men below the rank of oligarch, as well as organised-crime leaders. What unites them, says Borenstein, are money, a post-Soviet concept of labour, bad taste, conspicuous consumption, corruption and a lack of social conscience. This iden-tity has faded under Vladimir Putin.

The fourth Putin-era identity is the 'Orc', taken from J.R.R. Tolkien's *The Lord of the Rings* but representing a Russification of a Tolkien meme. The Orc is a malevolent creature, and Russians on different sides of the political spectrum use it to depict Russia's aggressive actions in its conflict with the West, particu-larly since the outbreak of war in Ukraine. Self-hatred, writes Borenstein, has been an integral part of unofficial Soviet and Russian identities.

The author describes Russia's war on Ukraine as an act of self-destruction, but also as a complex form of this self-hatred. After all, Putin has said that Ukrainians are not a separate nation and belong to Russia. How can one demonise a people that one claims do not exist? According to Borenstein, 'the Russian Federation's anti-Nazi rhetoric is the perfect corollary to its Nazi-style behaviour. Russia commits the crimes that match the label it uses to condemn Ukraine, all in the name of national greatness' (p. 162).

Belarusian Nation-building in Times of War and Revolution
Lizaveta Kasmach. Budapest: Central European University
Press, 2023. £64.00 288 pp.

Lizaveta Kasmach has written a comprehensive examination of the origins of Belarusian nation- and state-building during the First World War, contrasting how Belarusians living in the German-occupied part of the Russian empire (Ober Ost) conceived of their national identity with how those who lived in the empire itself did. She details how the Bolsheviks, who came to power having verbally committed to national self-determination, quickly extinguished the nascent independent Belarusian state. The proclamation of Belarusian independence in March 1918 in Ober Ost and the rival establishment of the Belarusian Soviet state in January 1919 'resulted in two distinct and mutually exclusive national myths, which continue to define contemporary Belarusian society' (p. 2).

Belarusians had lived in the Russian Empire since the collapse of the Polish–Lithuanian Commonwealth in 1795. This changed after Germany occupied part of the Belarusian lands during the First World War, leaving the other part under tsarist rule. Whereas the tsars had denied the existence of a separate Belarusian nation, dismissed their language as a dialect and introduced forced-assimilation policies, the Germans appealed to ethnic minorities under their rule and provided the Belarusians with new opportunities for nation-building. Belarusians established their own civic organisations, schools and aid societies, with Vilnius as the centre of their activities. The Germans encouraged them in these endeavours to weaken Polish influence. Until the February Revolution in 1917, when the centre of gravity of Belarusian activity shifted to Minsk, Belarusian activists achieved more in Ober Ost than their counterparts in Russia.

The fall of the tsarist empire opened up new possibilities for Belarusians in the non-occupied areas, but they faced two problems. One was the legacy of tsarist Russification policies, which militated against a separate national project. The other was the lack of a strong, structured organisation to advance the national cause. Moreover, the Belarusians were divided into different political factions, with many disagreements on how to pursue their goals.

In January 1918 the first Belarusian Conference opened in Vilnius to gather activists from the German occupation zone, to establish Belarusian national representation and to discuss the form of a future state. The following month, Germany and Russia began peace talks in Brest-Litovsk. Leon Trotsky refused to permit an official Belarusian delegation to attend, since Soviet Russia did not recognise Belarusian autonomy. In March 1918, the Belarusian Democratic Republic was formed on German-occupied territories, although the Germans did not support its establishment.

After Germany's defeat, Vladimir Lenin decided that a separate Belarusian Soviet republic would act as a buffer state in the west, and as a counterbalance to Ukraine and the newly independent Polish state. The Bolsheviks created the Belarusian republic to protect the new Soviet state. Throughout the twentieth century, independent Belarusian statehood was crushed, but, Kasmach argues, Belarusian nationalists succeeded because a new political entity appeared in Europe. This served as the basis for the creation of an independent Belarusian state in 1992.

Africa
Karen Smith

Architecture and Politics in Africa: Making, Living and Imagining Identities Through Buildings
Joanne Tomkinson, Daniel Mulugeta and Julia Gallagher,
eds. Woodbridge and Rochester, NY: James Currey, 2022.
£25.00/$36.95. 278 pp.

In *Architecture and Politics in Africa*, the contributors explore public buildings as sites where political identities, domestic politics and foreign relations are expressed and negotiated. Essentially treating public spaces as political texts, they examine not just the multitude of ways in which architectural spaces have been used as part of state-building projects, but also how they often take on alternative meanings that challenge the intentions of their creators. Employing an interdisciplinary approach, the volume reflects diverse methodological approaches and draws on different theoretical traditions in its analyses. The result is an empirically rich collection of cases, underscored by a sophisticated theoretical framework that allows for rich insights into power, agency, resistance and identity.

Showcasing the aims of the collected volume, Julia Gallagher and Yah Ariane Bernadette N'djoré explore citizens' understanding of the state in Côte d'Ivoire by examining popular discourses about the aesthetics of post-colonial state buildings. Focusing on a range of public buildings, including hospitals and presidential palaces, they show how these built spaces allow glimpses into the practices of statehood, in that they are places where policymakers make decisions that can enable or restrict the rights of citizens, and where ordinary people participate in state-making.

Innocent Batsani-Ncube uses the case of Chinese funding and construction of the Malawian parliament building to explore wider issues around China's influence in Africa. Treating the building not as an isolated act of benevolence by China, but as part of a larger phenomenon across Africa – Batsani-Ncube notes that, by the mid-2010s, China had financed the construction and refurbishment of 15 parliamentary complexes on the continent – the chapter delves into the motivations behind China's decision to finance and construct Malawi's parliament building. Daniel Mulugeta's chapter explores the Chinese-built African Union (AU) building in Addis Ababa, Ethiopia, and its ability to embody pan-African ideals. In conversations with officials and ordinary citizens in Addis Ababa and Abuja, he identifies tensions between different strains of pan-African thought, some emphasising formal, elite-led projects and processes of political and economic integration of African states, and others popular conceptions of African unity. In employing architecture to explore how the interactions between objects, actors, institutions and structures enable and constrain the imaginative process of constructing communities, he shows how perceptions of the building reflect both the possibilities of pan-Africanism and the AU's failure to deliver on those ideals.

All the chapters encourage the reader to consider more closely the function of public buildings as sites for reinforcing or challenging certain identities and embodying particular aspirations around modernity or tradition. Overall, the book succeeds in making a persuasive argument for foregrounding architecture in any attempt to understand not only Africa's politics and international relations, but the interplay between state and society, and domestic and foreign politics more generally.

Africa's Soft Power: Philosophies, Political Values, Foreign Policies and Cultural Exports
Oluwaseun Tella. Abingdon: Routledge, 2021.
£38.99/$52.95. 216 pp.

In this first book-length study of African soft power, Oluwaseun Tella focuses on the foreign policies of four key states: Egypt, Kenya, Nigeria and South Africa. Starting with the argument that existing definitions of soft power do not sufficiently capture all the elements of African states' soft power, the author deliberately sets out to 'de-Americanise' and 'Africanise' the concept. The conceptual chapter, however, instead draws on the examples of Brazil, Russia, India and China (the BRIC countries), concluding that, in addition to the sources of soft power mentioned by Joseph Nye, who first coined the term in the 1980s, trade, investment and aid should be understood as integral to soft power. The link between the soft power of the BRIC states, the African case studies that follow and the Africanising of the concept is regrettably not sufficiently elaborated. In a separate section, what the author terms 'African philosophies' – namely Pharaonism, Harambee, Omolúwàbí and Ubuntu – are outlined as offering significant potential as soft-power resources. While the values (such as collectivism) that are embedded in these world views offer alternative ways of thinking about interpersonal relations, the nature of society, democracy and development, their link to soft power is speculative, and they are discussed as one of many potential cultural resources rather than representing any kind of overarching framework.

In light of the author's aim of Africanising the conceptualisation of soft power, it is surprising that there is no attempt to situate the study within broader debates in international relations (IR) regarding Eurocentrism and the applicability of existing IR concepts to the Global South. Some engagement with relevant theoretical questions regarding the need for geoculturally specific concepts and theories, assumptions of difference and challenges to universalism, among others, would have positioned the study within the wider trend towards globalising IR. Despite the stated intention to move beyond Nye's definition, which is criticised for being based on the culture and liberal ideals of the United States, in the case studies the same elements that Nye emphasises (such as liberal democracy, the promotion of democracy and human rights) are used to assess the limitations of and decline in soft power of the states under discussion.

In all the chapters, the tension between the potential of culture to act as a soft-power resource and government policies (both domestic and foreign) comes to the fore. The strength of the chapters lies in Tella's attempt to explain the gap between the states' potential soft-power resources and their influence in international affairs. In particular, the sections on the constraints on the exercise of soft power make for an interesting overview of the respective countries' domestic challenges and foreign policies. While the philosophies are painted as having soft-power potential, some reflection on how they can also undermine it would have been useful. In the case of South Africa, for example, the government's stated commitment to Ubuntu in its foreign policy, emphasising a people-first approach and a sense of common humanity, often serves instead to highlight the inconsistency in its approach to global human-rights issues.

One of the main shortcomings of the book is its failure to clearly distinguish between potential sources of soft power (for example, in the form of cultural products) and actual soft-power projection. The result is that the chapters focus primarily on providing an overview of the cultural resources that these countries possess, without going into detail about how these are (or are not) translated into soft power. In addition, while the book provides interesting overviews of often under-recognised cultural resources and the multitude of constraints facing these states in exercising soft power, it does not succeed in its stated aim of Africanising the concept. Beyond being of academic interest, the book is also a reminder to African policymakers to pay more attention to the importance of soft-power resources as a strategic instrument in their foreign-policy toolkit.

Africa's Global Infrastructures: South–South Transformation in Practice

Jana Hönke, Eric Cezne and Yifan Yang, eds. London: C. Hurst & Company, 2024. £22.00. 313 pp.

Reflecting on the burgeoning literature on South–South relations, the editors of *Africa's Global Infrastructures* note that much of it is concerned with whether the emerging forms of cooperation between states in the Global South challenge the

Western liberal order and traditional development models. Instead of reinforcing perceptions of competition between different visions of global order, Jana Hönke, Eric Cezne and Yifan Yang prefer to use the term 'globalities' to refer to the myriad ways in which actors employ ideas and practices of the 'global' in their interactions. Emphasising the role of African agency in their examinations of Africa's South–South relations, the contributors provide analyses of a wide range of infrastructure projects that have resulted from Chinese, Brazilian and Indian engagement on the continent. Through in-depth empirical case studies of the entanglements between different actors, the authors show how ideas of the 'global' and of South–South relations are constantly being negotiated and transformed through a multitude of actors, processes and practices. Eschewing a state-centric, top-down approach, the emphasis is on practices taking place in large infrastructure sites (termed 'frontier zones'), including ports and railways. While the focus is on infrastructure projects, these are seen as being embedded in and reflecting a range of relevant relationships, and as also being, at heart, political projects.

The volume proceeds in three parts. The first includes chapters that explore the assumption that actors from the Global South, such as China, import models of development that challenge existing Western models. Raoul Bunskoek argues that there is in fact no definitive 'Chinese' model of development, and that, instead, alternative models are negotiated through interaction, suggesting a relational understanding of how new practices and orders emerge. The second part – which includes Jan Sändig and Jana Hönke's chapter on the role of advocacy groups challenging Chinese mining practices in the Democratic Republic of the Congo – centres on contestations, covering not just how African agency shapes the practices of Chinese, Brazilian and Indian actors, but also how civil-society groups in China, Brazil and India contest infrastructure projects in Africa. In the third part, on everyday entanglements, Elisa Gambino and Mandira Bagwandeen's contribution investigates labour relations in a Sino-African construction project, and asks whether and how Chinese labour practices are influencing infrastructure projects in Africa. In a thoughtful concluding reflection on the preceding chapters, Vineet Thakur encourages readers to eschew general analytical categories and to instead embrace the 'messy site of everyday encounter' (p. 223), with a view not only to drawing conclusions about the case at hand, but also to considering what broader theoretical insights can be gained.

In summary, *Africa's Global Infrastructures* goes beyond simple binaries of South–South cooperation as either challenging the Western-dominated global order or not, adopting a nuanced approach to exploring Africa's multiple entanglements with external actors through the prism of infrastructure projects. It also makes a contribution, albeit sometimes only implicitly, to our understanding of Eurocentrism in IR theory, and the tendency to think in terms of categories such as African, Chinese, Western and so on – constructed distinctions which, as the book reveals, are blurred in practice.

Africa Is Not a Country: Breaking Stereotypes of Modern Africa
Dipo Faloyin. London: Harvill Secker, 2022. £16.99. 380 pp.

Written in a conversational style with a healthy infusion of humour, Dipo Faloyin's *Africa Is Not a Country* pushes back against what Nigerian author Chimamanda Ngozi Adichie has referred to as the 'single story' of Africa and its dangers, providing the reader with multiple and diverse accounts that address the persistent stereotypes of the continent.

By reminding us that Africa comprises 54 countries, 1.4 billion people and more than 2,000 languages, Faloyin reveals the absurdity of the notion that the same stereotypes of poverty, conflict and disease apply to the entire continent. Without being naive about the tremendous challenges that Africa faces – stereotypes usually have some basis in reality, though they tend to focus only on a limited aspect of the larger truth – he also tries to provide some context for complex problems that are too easily dismissed based on simplistic and essentialist narratives. In eight parts, he engages with an array of topics ranging from dictatorship to cultural restitution to jollof rice, all the while drawing on history and popular culture. For example, in a chapter titled 'The Birth of White Saviour Imagery or How Not to Be a White Saviour While Still Making a Difference', the author criticises the way in which the global aid industry fetishises images of poverty and disease with the aim of gaining support for its cause, and how charitable intentions can serve to perpetuate harmful stereotypes. Using the 'Kony 2012' campaign, which sought the arrest of Ugandan militia leader Joseph Kony, as a case in point, he problematises the way in which complex situations are reduced to simple narratives. In other chapters he recounts often tongue-in-cheek anecdotes about authoritarian figures such as Somali dictator Mohammed Siad Barre and Libya's Muammar Gadhafi, and lesser-known political dynasties like the Nguemas of Equatorial Guinea, commenting on the role of Western powers in keeping these dubious characters in power. All this is done in an engaging, accessible style that is clearly aimed at a wider audience. The drawback of this approach is that, while the text is interspersed with bits of data and random facts, these are not backed up with references.

The discerning reader might question the utility of this book for policymakers and scholars in the field of security studies, but conflict and security are not separate from the everyday lives of people, nor from the perceptions of policymakers and publics that underlie international action, including humanitarian aid and intervention. Following Faloyin's line of thought, the international community's engagement with Africa continues to be driven by deep-seated, entrenched ideas about the continent. A consistent theme throughout the book is the way in which Africans have been deliberately sidelined from decisions with grave consequences for them, including the Berlin Conference of 1884. While this is true to a large extent, it can also be criticised for, in turn, overlooking the agency of African actors not only in shaping their own destinies but also in co-constituting the ideas and practices of the international system.

In the end, the book is perhaps less about challenging stereotypes and more about complementing the single story with a multifaceted portrait that weaves together history and popular culture.

Kenya's Engagement with China: Discourse, Power, and Agency
Anita Plummer. East Lansing, MI: Michigan State University Press, 2022. $49.95. 244 pp.

Set against the background of China's increasing importance on the African continent, *Kenya's Engagement with China* provides an Africa-centred analysis that avoids the usual centring of China. While there has been a proliferation of studies on China–Africa relations, those focusing on China's involvement in individual states are still in the minority, and it is to this literature that Anita Plummer makes a contribution.

In her work on African agency in the context of China–Africa engagement, Plummer is particularly interested in the tension between state-sponsored narratives and the counter-discourse arising from the collective and individual experiences of ordinary Kenyans. Unlike much existing work on African agency, which tends to be mainly state-centric or focused on the role of individual leaders, *Kenya's Engagement with China* instead gives voice to ordinary individuals and civil groups, whose micronarratives were gathered by the author through interviews and from traditional media and online sources. She contends that recognising and understanding these competing narratives is important not only because it constitutes a meaningful form of citizen engagement, but also because it 'articulates an alternative vision of political development processes' (p. xxv) that could influence policy, including Kenya's foreign policy towards China. Perhaps surprisingly, her finding is that critiques of Sino-Kenyan engagement are in fact more critical of the Kenyan government than of China.

The counter-narratives are set against China's public-diplomacy efforts and its strategies to influence public perceptions of Chinese engagement in Kenya, which are discussed in the first two chapters. These include an overview of the origin story of China–Africa relations promoted by official Chinese-government sources, which emphasises an 800-year history that is markedly distinct from the West's relationship with the continent, and, more recently, Afro-Asian solidarity. At the same time, it conveniently glosses over the contentious relationship between China and Kenya during the Cold War, during which then-president Jomo Kenyatta warned: 'It is naïve to think that there is no danger of imperialism from the East. In world power politics the East has as much designs upon us as the West and would like us to serve their interests' (pp. 15–16). Interestingly, the author finds that these historical framings have not influenced public discourse. The rest of the book examines critical reactions to top-down elite narratives on a range of issues, including industrial policy and trade, infrastructure, labour relations and employment, and environmental sustainability and justice. With regard to the latter, activists highlight the fact that while China is pursuing a green-development model at home, this same commitment is not reflected in its overseas activities.

Plummer draws on a rich array of sources including interviews, tweets, blog posts and music videos. By centring the agency of ordinary Kenyans, she shows how, in an era of social media, it is exceedingly difficult for state messaging and propaganda to remain uncontested. The book also makes clear that foreign policy is not separate from local realities.

Deterrence and Arms Control
Målfrid Braut-Hegghammer

Inheriting the Bomb: The Collapse of the USSR and the Nuclear Disarmament of Ukraine
Mariana Budjeryn. Baltimore, MD: Johns Hopkins University Press, 2022. $34.95. 310 pp.

The war in Ukraine, now continuing into its third year, brought nuclear weapons back to the forefront of international security. As Russia made nuclear threats in the first year of this disastrous conflict, another emerging debate centred on Ukraine's own nuclear past. What if Ukraine had pursued an independent nuclear arsenal following the demise of the Soviet Union, and what lessons will other states draw from Ukraine's decision to give up the world's third-largest arsenal in return for the hapless security assurances provided by the 1994 Budapest Memorandum?

In *Inheriting the Bomb*, Mariana Budjeryn offers rich and original insights into these pressing questions. The book draws on fascinating primary sources collected by the author through archival searches and interviews with relevant actors from several countries. She challenges the troubling narrative that Ukrainian negotiators naively agreed to terms that they later came to regret, while adding important nuances to our understanding of the Budapest Memorandum – in which Ukraine received security assurances, not guarantees, in return for its inherited nuclear weapons.

According to some assessments, Ukraine could have developed a complete nuclear-weapons programme within three to five years post-independence (p. 182). Despite Ukraine's capabilities and Kyiv's serious concerns about Russian intentions, Budjeryn argues that proceeding with a nuclear option was not politically feasible in the international environment of the early 1990s. As one senior Ukrainian figure put it, abandoning nuclear weapons was the price of Ukrainian independence. This was ultimately a choice reflecting the kind of state Ukraine wanted to become, as well as a condition of its emergence as such. The alternative would likely have meant closer alignment with Russia. That option appealed to some Ukrainian military figures, but rather less so to Ukraine's political leaders.

Revisiting these choices, the Ukrainian negotiators now feel betrayed by both Russia and the West. According to former president Leonid Kuchma, the Ukrainian negotiators were not prepared for a situation where 'promises at that level could be hollow, that such duplicity and cynicism were possible' (p. 229). It is difficult to avoid the suspicion that other states looking to this case are likely to reach similar conclusions.

Inheriting the Bomb is required reading for anyone engaging in counterfactual discussions about a nuclear-armed Ukraine. Budjeryn's book frames Ukraine's nuclear choices in their proper context, and provides important contemporary insights into how the Ukrainian elites themselves understood these options. The book is also an example of why nuclear history matters beyond the realm of academic discussions. After all, as Budjeryn demonstrates, states rarely make nuclear choices under conditions of their own choosing.

Atomic Steppe: How Kazakhstan Gave Up the Bomb
Togzhan Kassenova. Stanford, CA: Stanford University Press, 2022. $32.00. 384 pp.

Atomic Steppe addresses both the high politics and individuals' experiences of Kazakhstan's nuclear past and decision to become a non-nuclear-weapons state. The book draws on immersive research in relevant archives and interviews with those who participated in the negotiations leading to Kazakhstan's decision to transfer Soviet nuclear weapons to Russia. At the time of independence, the inherited arsenal of Soviet weapons would have made Kazakhstan the world's fourth-largest nuclear power. The young nation was concerned about facing both a nuclear-armed Russia and a nuclear-armed China. Given this, author Togzhan Kassenova asks why Kazakhstan did not become a Central Asian North Korea.

On the one hand, Kazakhstan had nuclear warheads and delivery systems, the world's second-largest uranium reserves, and testing sites. On the other hand, it did not have an independent military, strong state institutions or well-protected borders. Unlike Ukraine, Kazakhstan lacked pro-nuclear elites at key decision points. Its population had also mobilised against nuclear tests, and the national mood was characterised by 'nuclear phobia' (p. 262). While nuclear weapons were inextricably linked with Kazakhstan's emergence as a sovereign state, the nuclear issue was one of many pressing challenges facing the country's leadership.

Below the level of high politics, *Atomic Steppe* vividly recounts the rough and dangerous beginnings of Soviet nuclear testing, and the growing fear and resistance that emerged among Kazakhstan's population. The book refers to several accidental deaths among locals and conscripts working in the testing complex. In addition to illnesses and birth defects that many locals suspected were caused by the testing, suicide epidemics among the area's youth were also attributed to the tests. Even so, in the opening pages of the book, Kassenova notes that it is not possible to fully establish the consequences of the Soviet nuclear tests for the country's people and natural environment. *Atomic Steppe* reflects on what we can know about these consequences, and what we may never know, which in itself highlights the tragic consequences of this nuclear legacy.

Given all this, it is perhaps not surprising that the patriotic workers of the testing complex felt shunned and abandoned after independence, both by Russia and by Kazakhstan. Some were so angry that they destroyed even the bathroom sinks as they left. But not everything was abandoned. As Kassenova recounts, 'a witness recalled how the military burned, ripped, or stuffed documents into bags to be taken to Russia' (p. 259).

It is possible that more could be learned from these records. Then again, given the increasing sensitivity surrounding the issue of nuclear testing in Russia, this seems at best a distant prospect. *Atomic Steppe* may serve as the most authoritative account for many years to come.

Hinge Points: An Inside Look at North Korea's Nuclear Program
Siegfried S. Hecker. Stanford, CA: Stanford University Press, 2023. $40.00. 386 pp.

Hinge Points presents a first-hand account of North Korea's secret nuclear facilities as told by a leading US nuclear expert. It also provides a behind-the-scenes look at the mechanics of the US policy to curb North Korea's nuclear-weapons programme. Siegfried Hecker offers a refreshingly detailed (and, in one key episode, almost tactile) description of spaces few will ever enter, paired with a crisp analysis of lost opportunities.

The contrast Hecker draws between the dirt roads he used to reach North Korea's nuclear complex and the condition of the complex itself resonates with the oft-noted paradox of North Korea's nuclear success. This was a success that should have been a failure, according to many theories of nuclear proliferation that have since needed to be revised. In *Hinge Points*, Hecker makes clear through his precise description of his North Korean interlocutors and the settings in which he encountered them that they were frequently different from what he had expected to find. His book highlights the fact that misguided assumptions about authoritarian regimes can be both costly and dangerous.

Hecker unsurprisingly makes a strong case for the value of the kind of engagement in which he was involved. For example, he shows that his interactions with North Koreans were particularly valuable given their concerns about inspections followed by regime change in Iraq. While Hecker's visits to North Korea were carefully staged by his hosts, they nonetheless produced valuable information and opportunities to address misunderstandings.

A central lesson in *Hinge Points* is how to recognise an opportunity when it emerges, and to discern when the moment has passed. The US failure to connect technical assessments with political choices remains a frustrating theme. Hecker argues that North Korea pursued a dual-track approach pairing diplomatic engagement with the US with the development of a nuclear-weapons capability, but also that

> the Bush, Obama, and Trump administrations failed to see that strategy, much less to cope effectively with it. Their misguided assumptions and deep suspicions about North Korea repeatedly caused all three administrations to miss opportunities to mitigate risk and to alter the trajectory of the North's nuclear program during times when Pyongyang favoured the diplomatic track. (p. 352)

Libya developed a similar strategy during the 1990s with a rather different outcome.

One of the central obstacles Hecker encountered on the US side was the legacy of North Korean cheating. He recalls hardline US officials arguing that the North Koreans 'have cheated on every agreement they have ever signed, and they will continue to do so' (p. 117). This approach backfired, Hecker suggests, writing that 'when the Americans walked away from the Agreed Framework, they opened the door for North Korea to put the Yongbyon complex back in full swing and to accelerate the efforts it had been pursuing clandestinely' (p. 89).

Was there ever a real chance to resolve the North Korean nuclear crisis? Hecker's measured analysis suggests we will never know. However, his account of the trajectory from his own first visit to Yongbyon through to North Korea's emergence as one of very few states capable of threatening the United States implies, at the very least, that there were important missed opportunities along the way.

Euromissiles: The Nuclear Weapons that Nearly Destroyed NATO
Susan Colbourn. Ithaca, NY: Cornell University Press, 2022.
$36.95. 392 pp.

In *Euromissiles*, Susan Colbourn provides a transatlantic history that impresses both in terms of its scope and the clarity of its arguments and conclusions. The book is perfectly timed, coming after the demise of the Intermediate-Range Nuclear Forces (INF) Treaty (along with the broader arms-control enterprise as we have known it) and the re-emergence of nuclear threats in connection with the Russian invasion of Ukraine. It is a compelling, richly contextualised and vivid account of the origins of the 1979 NATO Dual-track Decision and subsequent developments culminating in the 1987 INF Treaty.

This engaging book calls for greater precision and care in how analysts characterise this history and the stakes involved. As Colbourn argues, there has been a tendency for scholars to 'almost instinctively use the language of crisis' while discussing the Euromissiles issue, whereas there is no apparent consensus about what made this a crisis (p. 4). She makes clear that there are strong reasons for being very selective in the language used, as 'repeated assertions of an alliance in crisis can obscure the fact that not all crises are created equal' (p. 267).

On the Western side, many contenders claim a portion of the credit for the seemingly ideal solution that ended the Euromissiles episode: the INF Treaty, which eliminated US and Soviet ground-launched nuclear and conventional missiles with ranges of 500–5,500 kilometres. As Colbourn's account reminds us, however, this outcome was highly controversial at the time. The author argues that 'what saved the Atlantic alliance was not the wisdom of its policies nor the strength of its arguments, but the fact that the [Warsaw] pact's problems turned out to be even more acute' (p. 260).

Euromissiles contains several insights that speak to ongoing debates about the future of arms control; NATO's future prospects in view of upcoming elections in the United States and Europe; and more fundamental questions about how to pursue and make sense of security in the nuclear age. These insights caution against the optimistic argument that crisis breeds important breakthroughs in arms control, and highlights the fact that the INF breakthrough was not a foregone conclusion.

This history also highlights the fragility of the NATO Alliance as a set of democracies facing an authoritarian adversary. As Colbourn argues, democracy was an 'easily exploited weakness' that 'could be harnessed to turn citizens in the West against their own governments – and against NATO' (p. 7). This vulnerability has come back into focus in recent years as Russian attempts to weaken NATO from within have received more attention in European elections, and as some advocates for the Treaty on the Prohibition of Nuclear Weapons have levelled criticism at European non-nuclear-weapons states for participating in NATO's nuclear umbrella. In the years prior to the Ukraine war, such arguments were gathering momentum in some European states. Whereas that tide seems to have turned, at least for the time being, *Euromissiles* reminds us that fundamental questions about nuclear deterrence and reassurance among elites and publics alike will remain challenging within an expanded NATO Alliance.

Managing U.S. Nuclear Operations in the 21st Century
Charles Glaser, Austin Long and Brian Radzinsky, eds. Washington
DC: Brookings Institution Press, 2022. $38.50. 301 pp.

In 1987, the Brookings Institution published *Managing U.S. Nuclear Operations*, which became an essential contribution for understanding both the details and the logic of US nuclear operations. In *Managing U.S. Nuclear Operations in the 21st Century*, an impressive roster of senior practitioners and scholars reflect on what has changed since 1987 and what remains the same. For example, John R. Harvey and John K. Warden point out that the United States' nuclear command and control system is 'fundamentally the same system that was in place during the 1970s' (p. 171). At the same time, cyber surveillance of the system now requires assuming both that the adversary will eventually gain access and that adversarial actors will have the same level of expertise as leading Silicon Valley computer scientists (p. 193) – a chilling assumption indeed.

The chapters written by practitioners with direct experience of key episodes and changes both during the 1980s and in the post-Cold War era provide valuable insights that are sadly often elusive in the literature. The book offers reflections on fundamental challenges such as the issue of credibility, and the tensions between the goals of establishing deterrence and preparing for its potential failure. A recurring theme is the changing mixture of civil and military contributions to nuclear planning and targeting during and after the Cold War. This includes sobering examples of flawed attack options generated during the 1980s in moments where 'data processing had triumphed over military analysis' (p. 63), and the frequent disconnect between the options the US president believed were available and those that actually existed (p. 65). The value of civilian input is emphasised (p. 87), as is the importance of ensuring discipline and motivation among key personnel following troubling examples of the opposite (p. 135).

Extended nuclear deterrence has become more complex and challenging since the 1987 volume was published. This is not only because of a more complex security environment, but also, as Elaine Bunn points out, because extended nuclear deterrence represents an extraordinary commitment, the nature of which is 'amazing from both extender's and extendee's perspective' (p. 219). Given that challenges to extended deterrence have recently resurfaced in NATO, this volume offers a timely reminder that what has perhaps at times been taken for granted is a carefully crafted, and ultimately fragile, enterprise.

Ukraine vs Gaza

John Raine

I

In autumn 2023, Ukraine's spring offensive ran up against the hard realities of Russian defences. Ukrainian President Volodymyr Zelenskyy was
hitting other obstacles, too, as his diplomacy felt the impact of shifts in
geopolitical trends favouring Russian President Vladimir Putin. They
included the rise in the strategic assertiveness of middle powers; the
strengthening of like-minded groups of countries who felt disempow-
ered under the post-Second World War dispensations; the promotion of
nationalist agendas; and a revalorisation of authoritarian government, of
which Putin was the arch-practitioner. That was before 7 October, when
Hamas's brutal attack on Israel and Israel's ruthless response dislodged
Ukraine from the top slot on the global-security agenda. While the course
and outcome of the Russia–Ukraine war remain unclear, the Gaza war has
undoubtedly fuelled geopolitical trends that compromise Ukraine's position and which Zelenskyy must contend with if Ukraine is to survive, let
alone win.

The wars in Ukraine and Israel are manifestly different in character
and seem to belong on split screens. One is a war of imperial conquest
waged by an expansionist military superpower against a sovereign state,

John Raine is IISS Senior Adviser for Geopolitical Due Diligence. This article was adapted from an IISS Online
Analysis that was published on 5 October 2023 at https://www.iiss.org/online-analysis/online-analysis/2023/10/
zelenskyys-race-against-geopolitics/.

 https://doi.org/10.1080/00396338.2024.2309086

the other the fight of a sovereign state against non-state actors and terrorists. But they do share common features and, problematically for Zelenskyy, certain dependencies. Both wars are being fought over sovereignty and territory. The United States and Iran are involved as suppliers of military assistance in each conflict. In both cases, vetoes have neutered the United Nations Security Council and rendered UN agencies powerless. Secondary similarities include the unusually high level of citizen forces mobilised in both Ukraine and Israel; the disruption of global liquefied-natural-gas supplies now that the Gaza war has drawn in the piratical Houthis; and a mediating role for the Arab Gulf states, in particular Qatar, a rising geopolitical entrepreneur.

The most important of these linkages is the cardinal role the US plays as security guarantor and armourer for Ukraine and Israel. Ukraine must now compete for military assistance and attention with the formidable Israeli lobby. American assistance to Ukraine has already become subject to congressional packaging and conditionality where there was none before. Donald Trump's MAGA supporters in the House of Representatives have managed, as of this writing, to block the Biden administration's request for new funding to support Ukraine's defence; as Trump's renomination as the Republican presidential candidate looks ever more likely, support for Ukraine among Republicans is likely to dim even further. If pressed to choose between defending Israel against terrorists and defending Ukraine against Russia, even for the sake of NATO, US politicians of both stripes will be inclined, especially during a presidential-election year, to follow the domestic votes.

The news for Ukraine isn't all bad. Its relations with the government of Israeli Prime Minister Benjamin Netanyahu have improved, and Putin's adoption of the Palestinian cause has increased tension between Russia and Israel. But Israeli sympathy for Ukraine, like any form of association with Israel, diminishes support for Ukraine among the nations – perhaps now a global majority – that are indifferent to Ukraine's fate and may gravitate towards Moscow for historical, commercial or political reasons, including in some cases long-standing anti-Americanism. In September 2023, Indian Prime Minister Narendra Modi did not invite Zelenskyy to the G20 summit and confidently steered the Leaders' Declaration in directions favourable to Russia. Next year the group's summit host will be Brazilian President Luiz Inácio Lula da Silva (Lula), the other flag-carrier for democracy among the BRICS countries, and he has said he will invite Putin. Turkish President Recep Tayyip Erdoğan may typify the policy fluidity of middle powers: he viscerally condemns Israel and, while formally opposing Putin as a member of NATO, has allowed Turkiye to function as a conduit for Russian commerce and delayed the admission of Finland and Sweden to NATO. Indonesia, the world's most populous Muslim country, reportedly declined to join BRICS, but has taken a leading role in supporting the Palestinians.

More ominously, Iran and North Korea, two regimes intensely focused on perpetuating their rule, have used the Russia–Ukraine war to leverage a deeper relationship with Russia. Saudi Arabia, South Africa and the United Arab Emirates (UAE), as well as Turkiye, have aligned with Russia to promote their own credentials as negotiators, bridge builders or, more ambitiously, regional or even global leaders. Putin meanwhile has seized the opportunity to skewer Kyiv by openly championing the Palestinian cause, which resonates in many Asian and African countries with strong institutional memories of colonialism. South African President Cyril Ramaphosa, a controversial but influential figure in that community, has backed Putin and the Palestinians, and brought a suit against Israel in the International Court of Justice alleging genocide.

II

This alignment will please Iran, a key disruptive actor in both wars and a new member of BRICS. Russia's Iranian-made drones are in constant use against targets inside Ukraine, and neither political recalculation nor new priorities for defence products has induced Tehran to recalibrate its support for the Kremlin. This could change if Israel follows through on its threats to take down Hizbullah as it has Hamas, which would oblige Tehran to concentrate resources on protecting Hizbullah. While Iran has avoided entering into direct hostilities as a state, it has remained involved in training and equipping the terrorist groups against which

Israel is fighting. By thus participating in both wars, Iran has upgraded its status as head of the so-called 'axis of resistance' to a leading role in a global community that increasingly opposes the US, NATO and the order they underwrite, but does not yet have a satisfactory alternative. What has emerged amounts to an 'axis of rejection' – a term earlier applied to Palestinian groups backed by Syria and Iran who rejected Yasser Arafat's Palestine Liberation Organization and any recognition of Israel. Their alternative of terrorism and political sabotage came to grim maturity on 7 October.

Iran is back in its groove as a regional disruptor and scourge-in-chief of the United States. It has secured the support, if not the protection, of Russia and China, while continuing to expand both its involvement in terrorism and, while eyes are elsewhere, the enhancement of its nuclear programme, all at relatively low cost. But this activity has brought a high degree of risk at a moment when Israel's tolerance for Iranian agitation is at a breaking point. Decisions that Iran's leaders take in the coming year on how they manage this exposure both in the Middle East and Ukraine, and how they deal with a faltering economy and a restless domestic opposition, will have material consequences for both wars. To add to the uncertainty, at some point soon the elderly Supreme Leader Ayatollah Sayyid Ali Khamenei will need to be replaced. There may be a seamless transition to an equally conservative senior cleric. It is also possible, however, that the edifice of an ageing revolution rejected by the young and unpopular for its foreign adventures comes tumbling down. In turn, Iran could find itself the swing player in two wars and the shaper of geopolitics among the global majority, or a chancer at the zenith of its influence from which it can only decline. Tehran's cautious avoidance of open conflict with Israel speaks to its fear that, for all its bombast, precipitating a shooting war would probably be the regime's last act. It values the threat of a showdown with Israel far more than it wants the showdown itself. Iran has structured its defence around a ring of regional non-state actors that provide both a defensive cordon and forward operating bases precisely because it is not equipped to defend itself against direct attacks by well-armed states.

Zelenskyy, for his part, cannot afford to wait for Iran or any other medium power to reorient geopolitics. The trends running against him are broad-based and gathering momentum. He will need to outpace two in particular: the increasing inclination of some US allies to de-link their own security strategies from those of the United States, and the normalisation of authoritarian power projection. The first has seen close US allies in the Gulf, in particular, seek to maintain deep defence and commercial relations with the US while pursuing strategically assertive foreign policies. Emirati and Saudi leaders have maintained openly friendly relations with Putin. They have also declined to join the US-led protection fleet in the Red Sea, though Bahrain, which signed a comprehensive security agreement with the US in November, is participating. The hazard for Zelenskyy is not so much outright hostility among the middle powers as it is the dizzying plurality of their security strategies. With the exception of NATO headquarters in Brussels, he has no one stop where he can shop for support in bulk. Moreover, winning support in Washington no longer guarantees the backing of non-NATO US allies. Russia and China have paralysed the UN. Even some of the NATO allies are nervous about sustainability. The wooing and dealing required to generate mass among international actors deeply divided on international security policy would exhaust a permanent member of the UN Security Council. It is even more to expect of Ukraine.

III

The Arab Gulf states have taken an independent line from the beginning of the war in Ukraine and will probably continue to do so. They are likely to be encouraged by the resilience of authoritarian power projection. Russia has been subject to an unprecedented level of US, European Union and market-driven sanctions, but it has generated record revenues from oil sales and reaped a war dividend in its domestic economy without disgorging the land it has taken from Ukraine or relinquishing its war aims. Its relationship with China, which at one point looked imperilled by Putin's costly miscalculations, has been reaffirmed by both sides. China, for its part, has absorbed the pressure of US policies, and continued to grow its armed forces and project its economic power. The authoritarian axis, along with the brand, is holding. It received a boost, if not a relaunch, by way of the expansion of BRICS at a summit in October to include leading middle powers in the Middle East and Africa.

However imperfect the expansion, BRICS now includes four top hydrocarbon producers: Iran, Russia, Saudi Arabia and the UAE. Buoying the enduring value of hydrocarbons are the adoption by parties to the 2023 UN Climate Change Conference of a watered-down resolution to phase hydrocarbons down rather than out, and steadily rising demand for Gulf-produced hydrocarbons in the Indo-Pacific. Meanwhile, Gulf states are insuring themselves against the long-term impact of the green transition on their hydrocarbon revenues with record investments in renewables and economic diversification. This hedging only increases their strategic confidence. It also bolsters the case for a *stabilitätspolitik*, towards which much Gulf diplomacy is directed. The unprecedented de-escalation starting with the Abraham Accords in 2020 and extending to the restoration of diplomatic relations between Iran and Saudi Arabia in 2023 reflect a shared disposition to balance the region politically in order to permit economic growth. Despite the political and humanitarian rupture of the Gaza war, that is likely to remain the Gulf states' objective. It will incline them to urge, or at least settle for, manageable ceasefires. On Ukraine, they represent many in the global majority. Their position on Palestinian statehood, which enjoys consensus international support, is apt to be more complicated.

In any case, they will not endorse maximal war aims in either conflict. In the rhetoric of Putin, Hamas and even extreme Israeli political leaders, the wars are portrayed as zero-sum games that entail the negation or triumph of existing political identities and entities. Ukraine remains absolutely determined to retain its territory and by implication to erase self-declared, Kremlin-backed political entities in occupied Donbas. While the international community includes fierce advocates of the principles of statehood and sovereignty, in practice compromises of both are usually required to end conflict. A desire to stabilise, if not resolve, the status of disputed territory will grow as the conflicts continue and casualties mount.

For Zelenskyy, two developments could reduce the pressure to compromise. The first would be if he could generate sufficient momentum in reclaiming occupied territory for his war aims to look achievable. The second would be for Europe and NATO to provide a critical increase in the type and duration of their military assistance. Since the two are reciprocally related, their appropriate sequencing is a matter of debate in Europe and Kyiv. Either way, to regain momentum, Ukraine and its allies will have to adjust a stalled strategy. That may well involve taking yet more risks militarily, as well as politically.

Israel's war will continue. So will its shadow over the Russia–Ukraine war. It may widen further, but it will remain asymmetric. Non-state groups may be drawn in further as targets or aggressors, as the Houthis already have been, but regional powers, including Iran, do not want to fight as states. If the current Gaza war mutates into a broader war involving Israel, and other states, against non-state groups across the region, that may help distinguish it in the minds of politicians and policymakers from Russia's war in Ukraine, which requires different resources and capabilities. Less helpful to Zelenskyy is the fact that whatever form its next phase takes, Israel's war is now an active ingredient in the evolving geopolitics that he and his supporters must navigate.

Printed in the United States
by Baker & Taylor Publisher Services